DETR

ENVIRONMENT
TRANSPORT
REGIONS

WITHDRAWN

Tree Preservation Orders

A Guide to the Law and Good Practice

March 2000

...ronment, Transport and the Regions: London

Department of the Environment, Transport and the Regions
Eland House
Bressenden Place
London
SW1E 5DU
Telephone 020 7944 3000
Internet service http://www.detr.gov.uk/

Further copies of this report are available from:

Department of the Environment, Transport and the Regions
Publications Sales Centre
Unit 21
Goldthorpe Industrial Estate
Goldthorpe
Rotherham S63 9BL
Tel: 01709 891318
Fax: 01709 881673

ISBN 1 85112 361 X

Printed in Great Britain on material containing 75% post-consumer waste and
25% ECF pulp (cover); 100% post-consumer waste (text).
March 2000

Preface

When the modern planning system was established under the Town and Country Planning Act 1947 local planning authorities retained their powers to protect trees and woodlands in the interests of amenity by making tree preservation orders. Over 50 years later tree preservation orders remain an important part of the system.

This Guide sets out the Government's policy advice on the tree preservation order system. It outlines the law as it currently stands in England, taking into account the Town and Country Planning (Trees) Regulations 1999 which came into force on 2 August 1999. It also suggests ways in which local planning authorities can run the system in line with good administrative practice. Authorities are not required to follow the advice given; the Guide imposes no new burdens on them. But for many authorities the Guide is a useful point of reference which is relevant to their day-to-day work.

The Guide is aimed at local planning authorities but has also proved a helpful source of advice for others interested in the tree preservation order system. Anyone relying on the Guide, though, should not regard it as a definitive statement of the law. The law is contained in the relevant primary and secondary legislation; this document is for guidance only. Anyone unsure of their legal rights or obligations should consult a solicitor.

Sections VI, VII, VIII, IX and X of Department of the Environment Circular 36/78 **Trees and Forestry**, in so far as they relate to England, are now cancelled. The Department's **Tree Preservation Orders: A Guide to the Law and Good Practice** (1994) is also cancelled.

Any questions about the Guide should be put to the Department's Rural Development Division, Zone 3/C5, Eland House, Bressenden Place, London SWIE 5DU (see Annex 1 for more details).

CONTENTS

CHAPTER 1

Introduction to Tree Preservation Orders

Their tallest trees are about seven foot high; I mean some of those in the great Royal Park, the tops whereof I could but just reach with my fist clinched.

– Jonathan Swift, Gulliver's Travels

TREE PRESERVATION ORDERS

1.1   A tree preservation order (referred to in this Guide as a "TPO") is an order made by a local planning authority ("LPA") in respect of trees or woodlands. The principal effect of a TPO is to prohibit the:

(1) cutting down,

(2) uprooting,

(3) topping,

(4) lopping,

(5) wilful damage, or

(6) wilful destruction

of trees without the LPA's consent. The cutting of roots, although not expressly covered in (1)–(4) above, is potentially damaging and so, in the Secretary of State's view, requires the LPA's consent.

LAW

1.2   The law on TPOs is in **Part VIII** of the **Town and Country Planning Act 1990** ("the Act") and in the **Town and Country Planning (Trees) Regulations 1999** ("the 1999 Regulations") which came into force on 2 August 1999.[1] The Act must be read in conjunction with section 23 of the Planning and Compensation Act 1991 which amended some of the TPO provisions in the 1990 Act and added four new sections (sections 214A, 214B, 214C and 214D).

---

1   Statutory Instruments ("SI") 1999, No.1892. The following Regulations have been repealed: (1) Town and Country Planning (Tree Preservation Order) Regulations 1969 (SI 1969, No.17); (2) Town and Country Planning (Tree Preservation Order) (Amendment) and (Trees in Conservation Areas) (Exempted Cases) Regulations 1975 (SI 1975, No.148); (3) Town and Country Planning (Tree Preservation Order) (Amendment) Regulations 1981 (SI 1981, No.14); (4) Town and Country Planning (Tree Preservation Order) (Amendment) Regulations 1988 (SI 1988, No.963); and (5) so much of article 2 of, and the Schedule to, the Electricity Act (Consequential Modifications of Subordinate Legislation) Order 1990 (SI 1990, No.526) as relates to the 1969 Regulations mentioned above.

GUIDANCE

1.3   This Guide brings together the Department's guidance and policy advice on the subject of TPOs. It replaces sections VI, VII, VIII, IX and X of DOE Circular 36/78 **Trees and Forestry** (in so far as they relate to England) and the first issue of this Guide, published in 1994. The status of this Guide is no different to that of a Government Circular, and so the weight attached to it should be no different to the weight that would normally be attached to a Circular.

LOCAL PLANNING AUTHORITIES

1.4   The power to make a TPO is exercised by the LPA. In England the LPA is the district, borough or unitary council. A county council may make a TPO, but only:

(1) in connection with the grant of planning permission,

(2) on land which is not wholly within the area of a single district council,

(3) on land in which the county council hold an interest, or

(4) on land in a National Park.[2]

1.5   Special arrangements apply in the following areas:

(1) in National Parks where the National Park Authority are responsible for TPO functions concurrently with the district, borough or unitary council;[3]

(2) in the Norfolk and Suffolk Broads where, again, the Broads Authority are responsible for TPO functions concurrently with the district, borough or unitary council. But so far as section 211–214 of the Act are concerned (these sections relate to trees in conservation areas: for more details see chapter 9 of this Guide), the Broads Authority are in fact the sole LPA;[4]

(3) in Enterprise Zones, Urban Development Areas and Housing Action Trust Areas, where the Enterprise Authority, Urban Development Corporation or Housing Action Trust are the sole LPA.[5]

When they make a TPO these authorities are advised to copy it for information to the tree officer of the district, borough or unitary council within whose area the trees or woodlands are situated.

2 See paragraph 13(1), Schedule 1 of the Act.

3 See section 4A(4) of the Act which was inserted by section 67 of the Environment Act 1995.

4 See section 5 of the Act.

5 See section 6–8 of the Act.

THE SECRETARY OF STATE'S POWERS

1.6   The Secretary of State for the Environment, Transport and the Regions ("the Secretary of State") has a power to make TPOs.[6] In considering requests to make a TPO the Secretary of State will have regard to all representations submitted to him, but it is likely that he would use his power in exceptional circumstances only, where issues of more than local significance are raised, and then only after consultation with the LPA in whose area the trees or woodlands are located.

6 Section 202(1) of the Act.

CHAPTER 2

Scope of Tree Preservation Orders

QUEEN MARGARET
They that stand high have many blasts to shake them,
And if they fall, they dash themselves to pieces.

RICHARD
Good counsel, marry! Learn it, learn it, Marquess.

MARQUESS OF DORSET
It touches you, my lord, as much as me.

RICHARD
Yea, and much more; but I was born so high.
Our aery buildeth in the cedar's top
And dallies with the wind and scorns the sun.

– William Shakespeare, *Richard III*

TREES AND WOODLANDS

2.1   A TPO protects trees and woodlands. The term "tree" is not defined in the Act, nor does the Act limit the application of TPOs to trees of a minimum size. Fruit trees, for example, may be included in a TPO provided it is in the interests of amenity to do so (see paragraph 6.17–6.19). The dictionary defines a tree as a perennial plant with a self-supporting woody main stem, usually developing woody branches at some distance from the ground and growing to a considerable height and size. But for the purposes of the TPO legislation, the High Court has held that a "tree" is anything which ordinarily one would call a tree.[7]

2.2   Neither does the Act define the term "woodland". In the Secretary of State's view, trees which are planted or grow naturally within the woodland area after the TPO is made are also protected by the TPO.[8] This is because the purpose of the TPO is to safeguard the woodland unit as a whole which depends on regeneration or new planting. But as far as the TPO is concerned, only the cutting down, destruction or carrying out of work on *trees* within the woodland area is prohibited; whether or not seedlings, for example, are "trees" for the purposes of the Act would be a matter for the Courts to decide in the circumstances of the particular case.

7   See *Bullock v Secretary of State for the Environment* (1980) 40 P&CR 246, where recently coppiced trees were held to be "trees" under the Act: "Bushes and scrub nobody I suppose would call "trees", nor indeed shrubs, but it seems to me that anything which ordinarily one would call a tree is a "tree" within ... the Act." (Phillips J.)

8   A view accepted by the Court of Appeal in *Evans v Waverley BC* [1995] 3 PLR 80.

HEDGES

2.3 A TPO may only be used to protect trees and cannot be applied to bushes or shrubs, although in the Secretary of State's view a TPO may be made to protect trees in hedges or an old hedge which has become a line of trees of a reasonable height and is not subject to hedgerow management. Separate legislation is in place to regulate the removal of hedgerows.[9]

CROWN LAND

2.4 A TPO may only be made for trees on Crown land[10] with the consent of the appropriate authority.[11] In most cases the "appropriate authority" will be either the Government department managing the land or the Crown Estate (see Annex 1). Section 300 of the Act makes special provision for the making of TPOs on Crown land in anticipation of that land being transferred to a private interest, although again the prior consent of the appropriate authority is required. A TPO made under section 300 takes effect provisionally as soon as the land ceases to be Crown land, but must then be confirmed by the LPA in the normal way (for guidance on confirming TPOs see chapter 3).

2.5 Before requesting consent to make a TPO, LPAs are advised to make telephone enquiries to identify the person or office responsible for managing the Crown land in question. Government departments have no objection in principle to the making of TPOs on Crown land, and their consent will not be unreasonably withheld. Any TPO made with the necessary consent applies only to those who hold a private interest in the land and does not bind the Crown. Nevertheless, Government departments will normally consult the LPA before carrying out any work which would otherwise require consent, and take into consideration any comments the LPA wish to make.[12]

2.6 Crown immunity from the planning system will be removed when a suitable legislative opportunity arises. This will include removing the Crown's present immunity from TPO controls. Provision will be made, however, to ensure that Forest Enterprise, the operating arm of the Forestry Commission, are treated in the same way as private landowners who manage their woodlands in accordance with an approved plan of operations, and that Crown bodies continue to be able to meet their statutory obligations.

2.7 Although crown immunity was removed from health authorities in April 1991,[13] immunity may in fact continue to apply in relation to land which is vested in the Secretary of State for Health.[14] NHS Trusts do not themselves have any crown immunity but, again, where the freehold interest in the land is held by the Secretary of State, crown immunity may apply. Before making a TPO on NHS land, therefore, LPAs are advised to consult the appropriate health authority and seek their consent where necessary. Health authorities will not unreasonably withhold consent, nor seek to defer consent pending disposal of the land.

9   See section 97 of the Environment Act 1995 and the Hedgerows Regulations 1997 (SI 1997, No. 1160). See also the Department's Guide, *The Hedgerows Regulations 1997: A Guide to the Law and Good Practice.*

10   "Crown land" is defined in section 293 of the Act. Church land is not Crown land.

11   See section 296(2)(a) of the Act.

12   See Part I of the memorandum to DOE Circular 18/84, paragraph 10–12.

13   Under section 60 of the National Health Service and Community Care Act 1990.

14   On 1 April 1996, for example (under the Health Authorities Act 1995), regional health authority land was vested in the Secretary of State.

THE FORESTRY COMMISSION'S "INTEREST" IN LAND

2.8   There are limitations to the making of TPOs on land in which the Forestry Commission have an "interest". The Act states that the Forestry Commission have an "interest" in land if, in respect of it:

(1) there is an existing forestry dedication covenant in force, or

(2) they have made a grant or loan under section 1 of the Forestry Act 1979.[15]

If (1) or (2) applies the Forestry Commission must give their consent before a TPO may be made.

2.9   The main grants currently available from the Forestry Commission for the planting, restocking or management of woodlands are under the Woodland Grant Scheme. In running their schemes the Forestry Commission have proper regard for environmental and amenity considerations, and proposals are assessed by reference to the UK Forestry Standard, incorporating Forest Guidelines, Forest Practice Guides and other standards of good forestry practice.

2.10   The LPA and the Forestry Commission should, where appropriate, liaise closely. If the Forestry Commission wish to accept an area of land into the Woodland Grant Scheme and that land is already the subject of a TPO, they will consult the LPA. If that land is subsequently accepted into the Scheme any felling in accordance with an approved plan of operations or working plan would override the usual requirement to obtain the LPA's consent under the TPO.[16]

2.11   For their part, LPAs must consult the Forestry Commission (see Annex 1) before making a TPO on land in which the Commission have an "interest", as defined in paragraph 2.8 above. If the LPA identify trees which they would have made subject to a TPO but for the Forestry Commission's "interest" in the land, they may wish to consider asking the Commission to let them know when that "interest" in the land is likely to cease.

LOCAL AUTHORITY LAND

2.12   LPAs may make TPOs in respect of their own trees or trees under their control. Sometimes they acquire land which is already the subject of a TPO. If the LPA (ie any department of the Council as a whole and not just their planning department) propose to cut down or carry out work on protected trees, they may grant themselves consent (for more details see paragraph 6.76–6.78).[17] In the Secretary of State's view it would very rarely be appropriate for one LPA to make a TPO for trees on land owned by another LPA in their area. Where such a TPO exists the latter would generally have to make an application to the former before cutting down or carrying out work on the trees.

---

15   See section 200(2) of the Act.

16   See section 200(3) of the Act.

17   See regulation 17 of the 1999 Regulations, which amends the Town and Country Planning General Regulations 1992 (SI 1992, No.1492), bringing to an end the requirement for LPAs to apply to the Secretary of State for consent.

CHAPTER 3

Making and Confirming Tree Preservation Orders

He found that in his rapture he had walked to the top of the garden. He stopped and looked down. His feet were ankle-deep in conkers, which had fallen overnight from the tree, the glossy fruit bursting from the spiky green shells. He knelt down and picked up two or three of the beautiful, shining things in his hand. When he had been a boy he had waited every year for this day. Now here was John, his boy, another chance.

He threw up the conkers into the air in his great happiness. In the tree above him they disturbed a roosting crow, which erupted from the branches with an explosive bang of its wings, then rose up above him towards the sky, its harsh, ambiguous call coming back in long, grating waves towards the earth, to be heard by those still living.

– Sebastian Faulks, *Birdsong*

POWER TO MAKE A TPO

3.1   LPAs may make a TPO if it appears to them to be:

"expedient in the interests of amenity to make provision for the preservation of trees or woodlands in their area".[18]

Amenity

3.2   The Act does not define "amenity", nor does it prescribe the circumstances in which it is in the interests of amenity to make a TPO. In the Secretary of State's view, TPOs should be used to protect selected trees and woodlands if their removal would have a significant impact on the local environment and its enjoyment by the public. LPAs should be able to show that a reasonable degree of public benefit would accrue before TPOs are made or confirmed. The trees, or at least part of them, should therefore normally be visible from a public place, such as a road or footpath, although, exceptionally, the inclusion of other trees may be justified. The benefit may be present or future; trees may be worthy of preservation for their intrinsic beauty or for their contribution to the landscape or because they serve to screen an eyesore or future development; the value of trees may be enhanced by their scarcity; and the value of a group of trees or woodland may be collective only. Other factors, such as importance as a wildlife habitat, may be taken into account which alone would not be sufficient to warrant a TPO. In the Secretary of State's view, it would be inappropriate to make a TPO in respect of a tree which is dead, dying or dangerous.

18   See section 198(1) of the Act.

3.3   LPAs should be able to explain to landowners why their trees or woodlands have been protected by a TPO. They are advised to develop ways of assessing the "amenity value" of trees in a structured and consistent way, taking into account the following key criteria:

(1) **visibility:** the extent to which the trees or woodlands can be seen by the general public will inform the LPA's assessment of whether its impact on the local environment is significant. If they cannot be seen or are just barely visible from a public place, a TPO might only be justified in exceptional circumstances;

(2) **individual impact:** the mere fact that a tree is publicly visible will not itself be sufficient to warrant a TPO. The LPA should also assess the tree's particular importance by reference to its size and form, its future potential as an amenity, taking into account any special factors such as its rarity, value as a screen or contribution to the character or appearance of a conservation area. As noted in paragraph 3.2 above, in relation to a group of trees or woodland, an assessment should be made of its collective impact;

(3) **wider impact:** the significance of the trees in their local surroundings should also be assessed, taking into account how suitable they are to their particular setting, as well as the presence of other trees in the vicinity.

Expediency

3.4   Although a tree may merit protection on amenity grounds it may not be expedient to make it the subject of a TPO. For example, it is unlikely to be expedient to make a TPO in respect of trees which are under good arboricultural or silvicultural management.

3.5   It may be expedient to make a TPO if the LPA believe there is a risk of the tree being cut down or pruned in ways which would have a significant impact on the amenity of the area. It is not necessary for the risk to be immediate. In some cases the LPA may believe that certain trees are at risk generally from development pressures. The LPA may have some other reason to believe that trees are at risk; changes in property ownership and intentions to fell trees are not always known in advance, and so the protection of selected trees by a precautionary TPO might sometimes be considered expedient.

MAKING THE TPO

Internal Procedures

3.6   Because TPOs are often made at a time when trees may soon be cut down or destroyed, many LPAs find it convenient to delegate the function of making a TPO to an officer or officers of the Council, and to put in place arrangements to act at short notice during and outside normal office hours. Members often retain the function of confirming TPOs, particularly where objections or representations have to be considered.

Site Visit

3.7   Before making a TPO the LPA officer should visit the site of the tree or trees in question and consider whether or not a TPO is justified. Any person duly authorised in writing by the LPA may enter land for the purpose of surveying it in connection with making or confirming a TPO,[19] although the LPA may in the circumstances decide to carry out the

---

19 See section 214B(1)(a) of the Act.

visit without entering the land. They may consider that the risk of felling justifies the making of a TPO before they have been able to assess fully the amenity value of the tree. This should not, however, prevent them from making a preliminary judgment on whether a TPO would appear to be justified on amenity grounds, nor from making a more considered assessment before the TPO is confirmed.

Preparing the TPO

3.8   A TPO must be in the form (or substantially in the form) of the model form of TPO included in the 1999 Regulations ("the Model Order").[20] If the LPA omit some of the provisions of the Model Order (such as the 2nd Schedule which provides, among other things, rights of appeal against the decisions of the LPA) the TPO may be so fundamentally flawed as to be ineffective.

3.9   The trees or woodlands to be protected must be specified in the 1st Schedule of the TPO and their location shown on a map which is also included in, or annexed to, the TPO. The scale of the map (ideally an up to date Ordnance Survey map) must be sufficient to give a clear indication of the position of the trees or woodlands (1:1250 will usually be sufficient for trees or groups of trees; 1:2500 will usually be sufficient for woodlands).[21]

3.10   The Model Order provides that trees may be specified:

(1) **individually** (each tree – T1, T2 etc – encircled in black on the map),

(2) by reference to an **area** (the boundary of each area – A1, A2 etc – indicated on the map by a dotted black line),

(3) in **groups** (each group – G1, G2 etc – shown within a broken black line), or

(4) as **woodlands** (the boundary of each woodland – W1, W2 etc – indicated by a continuous black line).

Any combination of these four categories may be used in a single TPO.

3.11   During the site visit the LPA officer should gather sufficient information to draw up the TPO with accuracy. The LPA officer should accurately record the number and species of the individual trees or groups of trees to be included in the TPO and their location (see also paragraph 3.14 below). In relation to areas of trees or woodlands it is not necessary for the purposes of the TPO to record the number of trees, and a general description of species should be sufficient. It is, however, important to gather enough information to be able to define accurately on the map the boundaries of the areas or woodlands in question (see also paragraph 3.15–3.18 below).

3.12   The LPA officer may also wish to record other information during the site visit for future reference such as the present use of the land, the trees' importance as a wildlife habitat and trees which are not to be included in the TPO. If resources permit the LPA may also find it useful to take photographs of the trees and their surroundings.

---

20   See regulation 2(1) of the 1999 Regulations.
21   See regulation 2(3) of the 1999 Regulations.

3.13   There is no requirement in the Regulations to describe the trees in the 1st Schedule and plot them on the map with pinpoint accuracy. But if a tree is cut down apparently in contravention of the TPO, the LPA may find it difficult to bring a successful prosecution if they cannot show clearly that the TPO relates to the tree it was intended to protect. A few examples illustrate the point:

(1)   a TPO is made in respect of T1, specified in the 1st Schedule to be an oak tree standing in the front garden of 20 Amenity Drive, and is shown encircled on the map. There is just one oak tree standing in the garden of 20 Amenity Drive as shown on the map. The TPO is clear and certain in its meaning;

(2)   a TPO is made in respect of T2, specified in the 1st Schedule to be an ash tree standing in the front garden of 22 Amenity Drive, and a circle is shown on the map. As it happens there are 3 ash trees in the front garden of 22 Amenity Drive. If the 1st schedule does not describe the tree in a way that clearly distinguishes it from the rest, the ambiguity should be settled by reference to the position of the tree shown on the map. But if the encircling line on the map is too loosely drawn, it may not be possible to ascertain with certainty which of the ash trees is protected;

(3)   a TPO is made in respect of G1, specified in the 1st Schedule to be a group of 10 beech trees in the front garden of 24 Amenity Drive. The group is shown to be within a broken black line on the map. However, there are 12 trees in the position described in the 1st schedule and shown on the map. Immediately, uncertainty arises as to which 10 of the 12 trees are covered by the TPO. If 2 of the trees are oak, the trees comprising the group of 10 beech would be readily ascertainable. But if all the trees are beech, it may not be possible to say with certainty which ones are protected.

Individual Trees and Groups of Trees

3.14   If trees merit protection in their own right, they should be specified as **individual** trees in the TPO. The **group** category should in general terms be used for trees whose *overall* impact and quality merit protection. The intention of the group classification is not simply to protect trees which have individual merit and happen to be standing close to one another, but for their merit as a group. The number of trees in the group and their species should be specified in the 1st Schedule of the TPO,[22] and if each tree's location can be indicated within the broken black line on the map, so much the better.

Woodlands

3.15   The boundary of the **woodland** should be indicated on the map as accurately as possible, making use of any natural landscape features or property boundaries in a way that will avoid any future uncertainty if trees close to the boundary are removed. Use of the woodland classification is unlikely to be appropriate in gardens. LPAs are advised to liaise with their regional Conservancy of the Forestry Commission before making a woodland TPO to ensure that the Commission do not have an "interest" in the land, as defined in the Act (see paragraph 2.8–2.11).

3.16   A woodland TPO should not be used as a means of hindering beneficial management work, which may include regular felling and thinning. While LPAs may believe it expedient, as a last resort, to make TPOs in respect of woodlands they are advised (whether or not they make a TPO) to encourage landowners to bring their woodlands into proper management

22   See regulation 2(1)(b) of the 1999 Regulations.

under the grant schemes run by the Forestry Commission. If, for one reason or another, a woodland subject to a TPO is not brought into such a scheme, applications to manage the trees in ways that would benefit the woodland without making a serious impact on local amenity should be encouraged (see paragraph 6.41 of this Guide).

Areas of Trees

3.17 Using the **area** classification (the so-called "area order") is an alternative way of specifying scattered individual trees. All the trees within the defined area on the map are protected if their description in the 1st schedule of the TPO is all-encompassing (eg "the trees of whatever species within the area marked A1 on the map"). The LPA may limit the TPO's protection to those species within the area which make a significant contribution to amenity, and this should be made clear in the description of the trees in the 1st Schedule (eg "the oak and beech trees within the area marked A2 on the map"). The area classification has its drawbacks. Firstly, it is possible that trees will be included in the TPO which do not merit protection. Secondly, unlike woodlands, the TPO protects only those trees standing at the time the TPO was made. Over time, as new trees are planted or grow within the area, it may become difficult to say with certainty which trees are actually protected. This is precisely the difficulty that arose in the Scottish case of *Brown v Michael B Cooper Ltd*, where a prosecution failed because of a lack of evidence that trees removed in 1990 had existed at the time the TPO was made in 1983.[23]

3.18 In the Secretary of State's view the area classification should only be used in emergencies, and then only as a temporary measure until the trees in the area can be assessed properly and reclassified. LPAs are encouraged to resurvey their existing TPOs which include the area classification with a view to replacing them with individual or group classifications where appropriate (see chapter 4 of this Guide).

Section 201 Directions

3.19 If it appears to the LPA that a TPO should take immediate effect they may include in the TPO a direction applying section 201 of the Act (a "section 201 direction"). The TPO takes effect on the date specified in the direction (which usually coincides with the date on which the TPO is made). But the TPO takes effect on a provisional basis only. It still needs to be confirmed by the LPA. If the TPO is not confirmed within six months of the date on which it was made, the provisional protection given by the section 201 direction comes to an end, although the LPA are not prevented from confirming the TPO after the six month period (see paragraph 3.34).

Completing the TPO

3.20 When completing a TPO the LPA should ensure that they:

(1) include the title of the TPO,

(2) include the name of the LPA,

(3) if necessary include the section 201 direction at article 3 of the TPO, not forgetting to insert the date on which it is to take effect,

(4) if necessary apply the TPO to any trees specified in the 1st Schedule which are to be planted pursuant to a planning condition,

---

23 See (1990) SCCR 675.

(5) complete the 1st Schedule of the TPO and the map in a way that does not give rise to uncertainty. The LPA are advised to enter the word "NONE" against any of the classifications in the 1st Schedule which are not used,

(6) check that the TPO is complete, including both parts of the 2nd Schedule and the map, and

(7) ensure the TPO is signed and dated.

It is up to each LPA to decide whether or not their TPOs should be sealed; the TPO legislation does not require the sealing of TPOs.

PROCEDURE WHEN THE TPO IS MADE

What the Regulations Require

3.21   Under regulation 3 of the 1999 Regulations, the LPA must, on making a TPO serve on the owner and occupier of the land affected by the TPO:

(1) a copy of the TPO, and

(2) a notice ("a regulation 3 notice") stating:

(i)   the LPA's reasons for making the TPO,

(ii) that objections or other representations about any of the trees or woodlands specified in the TPO may be made to the LPA,

(iii) the date, being at least 28 days after the date of the regulation 3 notice, by which any such objections or representations must be received by the LPA, and

(iv) the effect of the section 201 direction if one has been included in the TPO.

The LPA must also make a copy of the TPO available for public inspection at the offices of the LPA.

3.22   It is no longer necessary to copy TPOs to the District Valuer and Forestry Commission. However, LPAs are requested to send a copy of any woodland TPO that they make to their regional Conservancy of the Forestry Commission, on an informal basis.

3.23   The regulation 3 notice is an important document. It may be the first document the owner or occupier sees about TPOs (other than the TPO itself which is long and rather complex). The LPA are therefore advised to consider attaching to the notice some general information about TPOs, such as a copy of the Department's explanatory leaflet *Protected Trees: A Guide to Tree Preservation Procedures*.[24] The LPA should also briefly explain the procedures involved leading up to their decision on whether to confirm the TPO, as well as the name and telephone number of an officer who can give advice or answer any queries about the TPO. A model regulation 3 notice is at Annex 2.

---

24 Copies of the leaflet are available from the DETR distribution unit for free literature: tel (0870) 122 6236.

3.24   As mentioned in paragraph 3.21 above a copy of the TPO and regulation 3 notice must be served on the owner and occupier of the land affected by the TPO. This requirement extends not only to the owner and occupier of the land on which the trees are situated, but also the owner and occupier of any land **adjoining** the land on which the trees are situated.[25] This is a strict requirement: the documents must be copied to adjoining land in all cases and not just where, for example, the trees are overhanging the adjoining land. In the Secretary of State's view, the documents should be copied to the owner and occupier of land adjoining the parcel or parcels of land on which the trees are situated. "Adjoining land" here is intended to mean land which has a common boundary with the parcel or parcels concerned. It would not, therefore, be necessary to copy the documents to adjacent land on the other side of an intervening highway. The LPA do not have to copy the documents to adjoining owners and occupiers on the same date as they copy them to the owners and occupiers of land on which the trees actually stand. They need not delay making a TPO for want of information as to the identity of an adjoining owner or occupier. But when they copy the documents to the adjoining owner or occupier the LPA should bear in mind that they must allow that person at least 28 days to submit objections or representations in respect of the TPO to the LPA.

Serving Copies of the TPO and Regulation 3 Notice

3.25   The LPA may serve a copy of the TPO and regulation 3 notice:

(1) by delivering the documents into the hands of the owner or occupier,

(2) by leaving the documents at the usual or last known place of abode of the owner or occupier,

(3) by pre-paid registered letter or recorded delivery to the usual or last known place of abode of the owner or occupier.[26]

In the case of an incorporated company or body, methods (1) and (3) above may be used to serve the documents on the company's secretary or clerk at the registered or principal office.

3.26   When serving notice on an occupier of the land affected by the TPO or where the LPA cannot after reasonable enquiry ascertain the name of the owner of that land, the copy of the TPO and regulation 3 notice will be duly served if:

(1) they are addressed to the owner either by name or by the description of "the occupier" or "the owner", as the case may be, and delivered or sent in one of the ways specified in paragraph 3.25 above, or

(2) they are addressed and marked in a way that plainly identifies them as communications of importance and are:

(i) sent to the premises in a prepaid registered letter or by recorded delivery and are not returned to the LPA, or

(ii) delivered to some person on those premises or affixed conspicuously to some object on those premises.[27]

---

25 See the definition of "land affected by the order" in regulation 1 of the 1999 Regulations.

26 Section 329(1) of the Act.

27 See section 329(2) of the Act.

3.27   Where it appears to the LPA that land affected by the TPO is unoccupied, the documents and notice will be taken as duly served if they are addressed to "the owners and occupiers" of the land described by the LPA and are affixed conspicuously to some object on the land.[28] The LPA also have powers, for the purpose of enabling them to make a TPO or serve notices under the Act, to require the occupier or landlord of any premises to give them information about interests in the premises.[29]

Publicity

3.28   Other than the requirement to send a copy of the TPO and regulation 3 notice to people affected by the TPO, the LPA are not required to send a copy of the TPO to other local residents, authorities (such as parish councils) or groups. Where the interests of such residents, authorities or groups are likely to be affected or where there is likely to be a good deal of public interest in the TPO, the LPA should consider notifying them or displaying a site notice at a convenient place in the locality.

Making Objections or Representations

3.29   The purpose of requiring the LPA to serve a copy of the TPO and regulation 3 notice on the people affected by the TPO is to ensure they are all made aware of it and given a chance to comment on it. The regulation 3 notice must state that objections or representations about any of the trees or woodlands covered by the TPO can be made to the LPA. All objections and representations must:

(1)   be made in writing and delivered to the LPA (or sent so that, in the ordinary course of post, they would be delivered) by the date specified in the regulation 3 notice,

(2)   specify the particular trees, groups or areas of trees or woodlands in respect of which the objections or representations are made, and

(3)   in the case of objections, state the reasons for them.[30]

3.30   Objections and representations are duly made if they comply with (1), (2) and (3) above, or if the LPA are satisfied that compliance with those provisions could not reasonably have been expected in the circumstances.[31] If the LPA serve a number of regulation 3 notices on different people and on different dates, they should ensure that each person is given at least 28 days from the date of the notice to submit their objections or representations to the LPA.

3.31   Objections and representations can be made on any grounds, for example:

(1)   challenging the LPA's view that it is expedient in the interests of amenity to make a TPO,

(2)   claiming that a tree included in the TPO is dead, dying or dangerous,

(3)   claiming that a tree is causing damage to property,

---

[28]   Except where people affected have already given the LPA an alternative address for serving documents and notices on them: see section 329(3) of the Act.

[29]   See section 330 of the Act.

[30]   See regulation 4(1) of the 1999 Regulations.

[31]   See regulation 4(2) of the 1999 Regulations.

(4) pointing out errors in the TPO or uncertainties in respect of the trees which are supposed to be protected by it,

(5) claiming that the LPA have not followed the procedural requirements of the Regulations.

The LPA are required to take into account all duly made objections and representations before deciding whether to confirm the TPO.

CONFIRMING THE TPO

3.32 The LPA may confirm the TPO either:

(1) without modification, or

(2) subject to "such modifications as they consider expedient".[32]

On the other hand, they may decide not to confirm the TPO.

Internal Procedures

3.33 The decision whether to confirm a TPO which raises objections is usually taken by members. For TPOs which do not give rise to any objections LPAs may consider it expedient to delegate the function to officers of the Council. On the other hand, members may wish to confirm all TPOs where, up to the point of confirmation, the relevant TPO functions have been carried out by delegated officers.

The Importance of Confirming TPOs without Delay

3.34 The LPA should ensure they reach their decision on confirmation without undue delay. A TPO may include a section 201 direction which secures the protection of the trees on a provisional basis for up to six months from the date of the making of the TPO. The LPA should be ready to make their decision on confirmation before the end of this period. If they fail to make their decision within the six month period, they are not prevented from confirming the TPO afterwards. But they should bear in mind that, after the six months, the trees or woodlands lose the protection of the section 201 direction until the TPO is confirmed. In the event of a significant delay beyond the six month period the LPA should consider, before confirming the TPO, whether it would be more appropriate to make a fresh TPO, particularly if land affected has been newly occupied by people who were unable to comment on the original TPO.

Where No Objections or Representations are Made

3.35 If no objections or representations are made, and the LPA remain satisfied that the trees merit the protection of a TPO, they should confirm the TPO. If the LPA did not assess fully the amenity value of the trees when the TPO was made, they should ensure that they do so before confirming it (see paragraph 3.7).

32 See section 199(1) of the Act.

Considering Objections and Representations

3.36   If objections or representations are duly made, the LPA cannot confirm the TPO unless they have first considered them.[33] To consider objections and representations properly it may be necessary for the LPA to carry out a further site visit, which would in any case be appropriate if the LPA had not yet assessed fully the amenity value of the trees or woodlands concerned. Any objection or representation made on technical grounds (for example, that a tree is diseased or dangerous) should be considered by an arboriculturist, preferably with experience of the TPO system.

3.37   Discussion between the LPA and any person who makes an objection is encouraged. Discussion can lead to a greater mutual understanding of each side's point of view. This in turn can help clarify the main issues which will have to be considered by the LPA before they decide whether to confirm the TPO. Alternatively, discussions can lead to the withdrawal of objections.

3.38   Since LPAs are responsible for making *and* confirming TPOs, they should consider establishing non-statutory procedures to demonstrate that their decisions at the confirmation stage are taken in an even-handed and open manner. For example, the LPA officer could prepare a report for the committee or sub-committee that will decide whether to confirm the TPO. The report could include details of all objections or representations and the LPA officer's observations on these in the light of any site visit or discussions with people affected by the TPO. A copy of the report could be sent to those people who have made objections and representations, with an invitation to submit any further views before the committee meet to make their decision. The LPA could arrange for members of the committee to visit the site of the trees before making their decision. The visit could be followed by a hearing or inquiry back at the Council offices, where people affected by the TPO and the LPA officer are given a final opportunity to state their case.

Confirming the TPO Subject to Modifications

3.39   After considering objections and representations the LPA may decide:

(1) to confirm the TPO in relation to some of the trees specified in the TPO, but

(2) to exclude other trees from the TPO.

In these circumstances the LPA should confirm the TPO subject to modifications. The modifications must be clearly indicated on the TPO.[34]

3.40   Section 199(1) of the Act imposes no express limit on the LPA's power to modify the TPO at the confirmation stage. The Court of Appeal have held that the power to modify need not in principle be construed narrowly or strictly. Having said that, the Court went on to say that the LPA cannot use their power to modify a TPO so as to produce a "different animal". They cannot, for example, use the powers to change an area order to a woodland order, which would have the effect of producing a "different animal" by bringing within the scope of the TPO trees which grow or are planted after the date of the order.[35] Before using their modification powers at the confirmation stage LPAs are advised to have regard to this ruling.

33 See regulation 5(1) of the 1999 Regulations. LPAs should bear in mind that, since they are "both proposer and judge", ie since they are responsible both for making and confirming TPOs, "the obligation to deal thoroughly, conscientiously and fairly with any objection [is] enhanced" (see *Stirk v Bridgnorth District Council* (1997) 73 P&CR 439).

34 See regulation 5(4) of the 1999 Regulations.

35 See *Evans v Waverley BC* [1995] 3 PLR 80.

The Decision on Whether to Confirm: Endorsing the TPO

3.41   The LPA must make a formal note of their final decision on the TPO document itself. If they decide to confirm the TPO they must endorse it to that effect, indicating the date of the decision and whether or not the TPO has been confirmed subject to modifications.[36]

3.42   Even where the LPA decide not to confirm the TPO they must still record their decision on the TPO document.[37]

The Decision to Confirm: Informing People Affected by the TPO

3.43   As soon as practicable after confirming a TPO the LPA must notify the owners and occupiers of land affected by the TPO:

(1) of their decision and the date of confirmation, and

(2) of the time within which an application may be made to the High Court to challenge the validity of the TPO (ie six weeks from the date on which the TPO is confirmed) and the grounds on which such a challenge may be made (see paragraph 3.46 below).[38]

If the TPO has been confirmed subject to modifications, the LPA must send the owners and occupiers of land affected by the TPO a copy of the full TPO, as confirmed (ie not just a copy of the modifications), and a copy should also be made available for public inspection at the offices of the LPA, replacing the copy provided when the TPO was made.[39]

3.44   In view of the six weeks deadline for a High Court challenge, it is of the utmost importance that the LPA notify all people affected by the TPO without delay. The LPA should also give their reasons for the decision and explain its effect. A model letter is at Annex 3. The LPA should also consider notifying other people or groups who expressed an interest in the TPO or commented on it before confirmation.

High Court Challenge

3.45   The legislation provides no right of appeal to the Secretary of State against a TPO, either when made or confirmed. An appeal to the Secretary of State can be made, however, following an application to cut down or carry out work on trees protected by the TPO (for more details see chapter 7 of this Guide).

3.46   The validity of a TPO cannot be challenged in any legal proceedings *except* by way of application to the High Court.[40] An application to the High Court may be made by any person who is "aggrieved" by a TPO on the grounds:

(1) that the TPO is not within the powers of the Act, or

(2) that the requirements of the Act or Regulations have not been complied with in relation to the TPO.

To be "aggrieved" applicants should be able to show that they have a sufficiently direct interest in the matter.

---

36   See regulation 5(3) of the 1999 Regulations.

37   See regulation 7 of the 1999 Regulations.

38   See regulation 6(a) of the 1999 Regulations.

39   See regulation 6(b) and (c) of the 1999 Regulations.

40   See section 284 of the Act for the rule and section 288 for provisions about applying to the High Court.

3.47   An application must be made within six weeks from the date of confirmation of the TPO. The High Court may quash the TPO or suspend its operation wholly or in part. Failure by the LPA to comply with the requirements of the Act or Regulations may not be sufficient for the Court to quash the TPO; the Court should also be satisfied that the interests of the applicant have been "substantially prejudiced" as a result; any would-be applicant may first wish to consider whether the LPA's decision would have been more favourable if made in accordance with the statutory requirements.

3.48   Anyone thinking about making an application to the High Court is advised to take legal advice on the procedures involved and the likely costs that might be incurred if the application failed.

ACCESSIBILITY OF TPOs

3.49   A TPO is a charge on the land on which the trees are situated, and as such should be recorded promptly in the local land charges register.[41] The LPA are required to make a copy of the TPO available at their offices for public inspection at all reasonable hours, free of charge.[42] In the Secretary of State's view, LPAs should also be able to let members of the public know, over the telephone, whether or not particular trees are the subject of a TPO or situated in a conservation area within 48 hours.

---

41 A TPO is not a charge on land adjoining the land on which the trees are situated.

42 See regulations 3(3) and 6(c) of the 1999 Regulations.

CHAPTER 4

Varying and Revoking Tree Preservation Orders

The brothers had to drive through the woods to reach the meadows. Sergey Ivanovitch was all the while admiring the beauty of the woods, which were a tangled mass of leaves, pointing out to his brother now an old lime tree on the point of flowering, now the young shoots of this year's saplings brilliant with emerald. Konstantin Levin did not like talking and hearing about the beauty of nature. Words for him took away the beauty of what he saw.

– Leo Tolstoy, *Anna Karenina*

THE POWER TO VARY OR REVOKE A TPO

4.1   LPAs have powers to vary or revoke their TPOs.[43] The 1999 Regulations include new provisions on the procedures involved.[44] LPAs can use these procedures to vary or revoke any of their TPOs, including those which were made before the 1999 Regulations came into force.

WHEN TO VARY OR REVOKE

4.2   LPAs are advised to keep their TPOs under review. By making full use of their variation and revocation powers LPAs can ensure their TPOs are brought up to date when the time is right to do so. There are a number of reasons why, over time, it may become desirable to vary or revoke a TPO. Some examples are given below.

Changes to the Legislation

4.3   The TPO may have been made before the implementation of important changes to the Model Order. For example, TPOs made and confirmed before 1975 prohibited the cutting down, topping, lopping or wilful destruction of trees. They did not prohibit the "uprooting" or "wilful damage" of trees because these acts were not included in the Model Order until 12 March 1975. If the LPA have not yet varied their TPOs preceding this date to ensure they cover uprooting and wilful damage, they should consider doing so.

Geographical Changes

4.4   Some TPOs which are still in force were made as long ago as the 1940s and 1950s. In many cases the use of the land might have changed; the land might have been developed; trees standing at the time the TPO was made might have been removed (with or without the consent of the LPA); some of the trees still standing, perhaps, no longer merit the protection of the TPO; new trees might have been planted which do merit protection; the map attached to the original TPO might bear little comparison with a modern map of the area.

---

43   See sction 333(7) of the Act; see also Schedule 1, paragraph 13(2).

44   See regulations 8 and 9 of the 1999 Regulations.

4.5 Such difficulties are likely to be compounded when dealing with an old "area order", which protects only those trees standing at the time the TPO was made but does not identify each one. In time this is likely to lead to uncertainty about whether particular trees were present at the time of the making of the TPO (see paragraph 3.17). If it is no longer possible, by reference to the TPO and map, to ascertain with certainty which trees on the site are protected it may well be time to vary or revoke the TPO.

4.6 These difficulties are not necessarily reserved for older TPOs. TPOs are often made on land which is developed shortly afterwards. When the development is complete it may well be desirable to vary or revoke the TPO.

Errors

4.7 Errors in the 1st Schedule of the TPO or on the map may come to light after the TPO has been confirmed, though the period allowed for the making of objections and representations before confirmation should ensure that errors are kept to a minimum. When an error comes to light the LPA should consider using their variation or revocation powers to put it right.

REVOKING TPOs: PROCEDURE

4.8 To revoke a TPO the LPA must:

(1) make a formal order revoking the TPO (the "revocation order"),[45]

(2) endorse (or stamp) the original TPO stating that it has been revoked, including the date of the revocation order,

(3) send a copy of the revocation order to the people affected by the TPO (ie not only the owner and occupier of the land on which the trees stand, but also the owner and occupier of any land adjoining the land on which the trees stand),

(4) withdraw the copy of the TPO which is kept available at the Council offices for public inspection.

4.9 The revocation order takes immediate effect. Before revoking a TPO the LPA are not required to publicise their intention to do so or consult local people or groups. The LPA may decide that some form of publicity should take place, depending on the particular circumstances of the case.

VARYING TPOs: PROCEDURE

4.10 When varying a TPO the LPA's procedure will depend on whether new trees or woodlands are being added to the TPO.

---

45 No model revocation order is included in this Guide. It should be a short, uncomplicated document, identifying the TPO and giving the date of its revocation.

4.11   If the LPA want to vary the TPO in such a way that *no new trees or woodlands are added* to the TPO they must:

(1) make a formal order varying the TPO (the "variation order"),[46]

(2) endorse (or stamp) the original TPO stating that it has been varied, including the date of the variation order,

(3) send a copy of the variation order to the people affected and explain its effect. Only the owner and occupier of the land *affected by the variation* are covered by this requirement (including the owner and occupier of adjoining land),

(4) make a copy of the variation order available for public inspection at the offices of the LPA.[47]

A variation order in these circumstances takes immediate effect. Before varying the TPO the LPA are not required to publicise their proposals or consult local people or groups. But as with revocation orders (see paragraph 4.9 above) the LPA may decide that some form of publicity should take place, depending on the particular circumstances of the case.

4.12   If, on the other hand, the LPA want to vary the TPO so that *new trees or woodlands are added* to the TPO, they must:

(1) make a formal order varying the TPO (the "variation order"),

(2) serve on the people affected by the variation order (ie only the owner and occupier of the land affected by the variation, including the owner and occupier of adjoining land):

(i) a copy of the variation order, and

(ii) a notice stating:

(a) the LPA's reasons for making the variation order,

(b) that objections or other representations about the variations to the TPO may be made to the LPA,

(c) the date by which any objections or representations must be received by the LPA,

(3) make a copy of the variation order available for public inspection at the offices of the LPA.[48]

---

46 Again, no model variation order is included in this Guide. As well as identifying the TPO and including the date of its variation, it should indicate how the TPO has been varied, for example by attaching a copy of the TPO with the variations clearly indicated.

47 See regulation 8(1) of the 1999 Regulations.

48 See regulation 8(2) of the 1999 Regulations.

4.13   When adding new trees and woodlands to the TPO the procedure mirrors that for the making of a TPO in the first place. People affected by the variation order are given an opportunity to object or make representations. The LPA decide whether or not the variation order should be confirmed and cannot confirm it without first considering any objections and representations duly made. If they decide to confirm the variation order they must:

(1) endorse (or stamp) the original TPO recording their decision to confirm the variation order, including the date of the decision,

(2) notify the people affected by the variation order of their decision and the date on which it was made. If the variation order is confirmed subject to modifications a copy of the order as modified should also be sent to these people,

(3) notify the people affected by the variation order of the time allowed to challenge the validity of the variation order (ie within six weeks from the date of their decision) and the grounds on which such a challenge may be made (these grounds are the same as those described in paragraph 3.46),

(4) make a copy of the confirmed variation order available for public inspection at the offices of the LPA, replacing the copy provided when the variation order was first made.

4.14   Even if the LPA decide *not to confirm* the variation order they must still:

(1) endorse (or stamp) the original TPO, recording the LPA's decision not to confirm the variation order, including the date of the decision,

(2) notify the people who were affected by the variation order of their decision and the date on which it was made,

(3) withdraw from public inspection the copy of the variation order which was made available when it was first made.

PRACTICAL MATTERS

4.15   The LPA may wish to revoke a TPO and at the same time make a new one to take its place. For example, the LPA may wish to replace their "area orders" with new TPOs specifying the trees to be protected individually or in groups. In the case of a large area it may not be practicable to replace the TPO in one go; it should not be revoked at the outset, but varied in stages (by deleting successive parts of the area) until full revocation becomes practicable; and new TPOs should be made to replace each deleted part of the original TPO.

4.16   When exercising these powers, the LPA will wish to ensure that the date on which any new TPO takes effect coincides with the date on which the old TPO is varied or revoked. They will also wish to bear in mind any "unfinished business" that is yet to be discharged under the old TPO. For example, the LPA might have granted consent under the TPO subject to a condition that a replacement tree is planted; the determination of an appeal to the Secretary of State in respect of a tree covered by the TPO might be outstanding;

or the LPA might have issued a notice under section 207 of the Act requiring the replacement of a tree protected by the TPO. LPAs are advised to discharge unfinished business before revoking a TPO, or to vary only those parts of a TPO for which there is no unfinished business to be discharged.

4.17   As mentioned in paragraph 4.2 LPAs are advised to keep their TPOs under review. In particular they are advised to put in place a programme for reviewing the "area orders" for which they are responsible. A programme of work might be phased over a period of years depending on the number and size of the area orders currently in force. LPAs may find it useful first to compile a list of their area orders, bearing in mind of course that one TPO may include more than one area designation. In compiling such a list it may be worth recording the date of each area order, a rough-and-ready assessment of its size (large, medium or small), its location (residential, open space, parkland) and whether or not it is situated in a conservation area. A list of this kind should help the LPA put together a programme of review and an initial assessment of how long such a programme might take.

4.18   When reviewing area orders LPAs are advised not to make detailed assessments of the amenity value of every tree within the boundary of the area. They are advised instead to adopt a selective approach, to concentrate on trees and groups of trees which make a significant impact on the local environment and its enjoyment by the public at large. Depending on the amount of work involved in their review programme they might also decide not to assess trees which, if removed from the TPO, would still be subject to other controls. Trees in conservation areas, for example, if removed from an area order would remain subject to the controls described in chapter 9 of this Guide; and some trees, if removed from an area order, would remain subject to the controls of the Forestry Act (although these controls extend only to the felling of trees and do not at all extend to trees in gardens: see paragraph 6.30 for more details).

CHAPTER 5

Trees and Development

I took him around the garden, pointing out tasks that need to be done.
"Pruning, for instance," I said. "Do you know how to prune?"
He shook his head. No, he didn't know how to prune. Or didn't want to.
"Anyhow, do what you can to bring it back under control," I said. "So that it doesn't become a complete wilderness."
"Why?" he said.
"Because that is how I am," I said. "Because I don't mean to leave a mess behind."
He shrugged, smiling to himself.

– J M Coetzee, *Age of Iron*

TREES AND THE PLANNING SYSTEM

5.1   This chapter gives advice on the measures LPAs should take to secure the protection and planting of trees and other landscaping when considering applications for planning permission. The impact of new building development is generally enhanced (or mitigated) where adequate landscaping proposals are implemented, and so this should be given due consideration when applications for planning permission are submitted. Landscaping should be designed to complement the development without reducing the occupiers' enjoyment, so reasonable daylighting and other requirements should be observed.

5.2   The approach LPAs take in deciding whether to grant planning permission for development is set out in sections 70(2) and 54A[49] of the Act. Section 70(2) requires the LPA to have regard to the development plan (so far as it is material to the planning application) and any other "material considerations".[50] Where the development plan is material to the application, section 54A requires the application to be determined in accordance with the development plan unless material considerations indicate otherwise. LPA tree officers who deal with TPOs are strongly advised to maintain close links with their colleagues who deal with applications to develop land, as well as development plans and the enforcement of planning control.

5.3   Development plans set out the main considerations on which planning applications are decided. In particular, plans should seek to reconcile the demand for development and the protection of the natural and built environment, and so have a key role to play in contributing to the Government's strategy for sustainable development. The Government's guidance on development plans is set out in Planning Policy Guidance Note 12.

5.4   LPAs must include in their plans land use and development policies designed to secure the conservation of natural beauty and amenity of the land. Plans should not, however, include policies which are unrelated to the development or use of land. They should not therefore include the LPA's policies for deciding applications for consent under a TPO; but they

---

49   Inserted by section 26 of the Planning and Compensation Act 1991.

50   For more guidance on what is meant by "material considerations", see paragraph 50–56 of PPG1.

should include policies on measures that the LPA will take, when dealing with applications to develop land, to protect trees and other natural features and provide for new tree planting and landscaping.

5.5   Whether or not specific tree policies are included in development plans, the effect of a proposed development on trees and other landscape features is a material consideration. The Act places a *duty* on LPAs, where appropriate, to ensure they make adequate provision for the preservation and planting of trees when granting planning permission by imposing conditions and making TPOs.[51]

PRE-APPLICATION

5.6   In certain circumstances LPAs may consider it expedient in the interests of amenity to make a TPO to protect trees on land before a planning application is made. In doing so, they may wish to consider preparing separate guidance for potential developers giving an indication of the LPA's design expectations, drawing on any wider tree strategy of the LPA. The nature of such guidance would depend on the characteristics of the site but might usefully include a landscape survey together with an assessment of the trees both on and adjoining the site (using, perhaps, the assessment criteria in British Standard 5837: 1991, Guide for Trees in Relation to Construction), and a note about opportunities for tree planting. Such guidance should concentrate on general principles rather than detailed prescription.

PLANNING APPLICATIONS

5.7   It will often be helpful to discuss with developers the extent and form of any proposed development before a formal application is made to ensure it fits in with the LPA's expectations. Due consideration should be given to the landscaping of the site as well as the protection and planting of trees. Planning Policy Guidance Note 1 makes clear that good design should be the aim of all those involved in the planning process, and that landscape design should be considered as an integral part of urban design, since the appearance and treatment of spaces between and around buildings is often of comparable importance to the buildings themselves.[52]

Full Planning Permission

5.8   Applications for planning permission must be made on a form provided by the LPA, together with a site plan and such other plans and drawings necessary to describe the development.[53] Where an application is made for full planning permission the LPA may require the applicant to supply further information, including plans and drawings.[54] LPAs should not request more information than they need to reach a decision. For their part, applicants should ensure that applications are properly presented containing all the information needed for a decision, and they should provide additional information promptly when reasonably requested.

---

51   See section 197.

52   See paragraph 14–15 and Annex A.

53   See regulation 3(1) of the Town and Country Planning (Applications) Regulations 1988, Statutory Instruments 1988, No.1812.

54   Ibid, regulation 4.

5.9   The LPA should obtain an accurate site plan showing the proposed siting of structures, the existing contours of the ground and any proposed alterations in ground level. The plan should provide details of all existing trees including their crown spread, indicating those to be retained and those to be felled. Areas to be set aside for new planting should also be shown. In addition, the LPA may require details of trees and other landscape features on land adjacent to the development site which might be affected by the development or might be useful for screening or other purposes. Further detailed guidance is given in British Standard 5837:1991, Guide for Trees in Relation to Construction.

5.10   The LPA may find it useful to place the trees on the site into the following categories, as outlined in British Standard 5837:

(1) those whose retention is most desirable;

(2) those whose retention is desirable;

(3) those which could be retained; and

(4) those not worth retaining.

5.11   As well as assessing the amenity value of the trees as they stand, a range of other factors will need to be considered, including:

(1) the size and position of the trees as envisaged after the development, taking into account future growth. The proximity of trees to buildings is an important consideration because:

    (i) of the potential damage that a tree may cause to buildings, particularly on clay soils, unless precautions are taken in the design of foundations, and

    (ii) incoming occupiers of properties will want trees to be in harmony with their surroundings without casting excessive shade or otherwise unreasonably interfering with their prospects of reasonably enjoying their property. Layouts may require careful adjustment to prevent trees from causing unreasonable inconvenience, leading inevitably to requests for consents to fell. Also important is the proximity of utility services to trees; LPAs should ensure that they find out at an early stage where services are to be routed,

(2) whether effective provision can be made to secure the trees' protection during development operations. Sufficient space will be needed to enable the development to be carried out, for example for access, scaffolding, site huts, plant and machinery and storage,

(3) whether the trees can withstand the proposed changes in site conditions. They may, for example, be more liable to wind throw or wind snap if nearby trees are removed.

These matters are likely to require competent arboricultural or design advice.

Outline Planning Permission

5.12   An applicant who proposes to carry out building operations may choose to apply for outline planning permission. Outline permission requires the subsequent approval of "reserved matters" which relate to certain details of the development such as siting of buildings, access and landscaping. An applicant can, however, choose to submit as part of an outline application details of some reserved matters, and the LPA must treat them as part of the application to be decided at the outline stage; they cannot reserve them for later approval.

5.13   It is for the LPA to decide whether or not an application for outline permission should be considered separately from the reserved matters. If they believe an application cannot in the circumstances be considered separately from, say, the landscaping details, they may within one month of receiving the application notify the applicant accordingly and specify the further details they require.[55] Before granting outline permission the LPA are advised to consider carefully, in consultation with the LPA's tree officer, its likely effect on their ability to provide for the protection and planting of trees when dealing with the reserved matters later.[56]

5.14   When granted, outline permission cannot be withdrawn except by a revocation order under section 97 of the Act. The LPA should, where possible, attach notes to an outline permission to give the developer guidance on the form of development that would be acceptable to them. An application for the approval of reserved matters must include such particulars, and be accompanied by such plans and drawings, as are necessary to deal with the matters reserved.[57] The only conditions that can be imposed when reserved matters are approved are conditions that relate directly to those matters.

Consulting the Forestry Commission

5.15   The LPA's regional Conservancy of the Forestry Commission should be consulted on any development proposals which affect ancient semi-natural woodland. The types of proposal where the Commission wish to be consulted are those where any part of the development site:

(1)   consists of ancient semi-natural woodland or ancient replanted woodland recorded in English Nature's Provisional Inventory of Ancient Woodland;[58] or

(2)   is within 500 metres of an ancient semi-natural woodland or ancient replanted woodland, and where the development would involve erecting a new building or extending the footprint of an existing building.

The Commission's main interest in the second of these categories relates to the effect of the proposed development on the continuing viability and health of the woodland. Where the LPA are unclear whether to consult on a particular proposal, they should ask their regional Conservancy of the Forestry Commission.

---

55   See article 3(2) of the Town and Country Planning (General Development Procedure) Order 1995 (SI 1999, No.419).

56   For more guidance about conditions relating to outline permissions, see paragraph 43–47 of DOE Circular 11/95.

57   See article 4(b) of the Town and Country Planning (General Development Procedure) Order 1995.

58   Copies of the county-based inventories should already be held by LPAs, but further copies are available from local offices of English Nature and regional Conservancies of the Forestry Commission (see Annex 1).

PLANNING CONDITIONS

5.16   The LPA's ability to impose conditions on a planning permission enables many development proposals to proceed which would otherwise be refused. The sensitive use of conditions can improve the quality of development control and enhance public confidence in the planning system. In the Secretary of State's view, planning conditions should only be imposed where they are both necessary and reasonable, as well as enforceable, precise and relevant both to planning and to the development to be permitted.

5.17   The Department's advice on the use of conditions is in DOE Circular 11/95, which contains model conditions on the protection and planting of trees.[59] The use of model conditions can improve consistency, speed up the process of dealing with applications and save resources. But there is also a danger of using them as a matter of routine. They should therefore be tailored where appropriate to meet the individual requirements of each case.

Protection of Trees

5.18   Damage to trees can occur all too easily on development sites, for example by root severance during excavations (whether for buildings or underground services), soil compaction by vehicles or materials, the raising or lowering of soil levels, fires, careless contact with plant and equipment, spillage of chemicals etc. When granting outline planning permission, the LPA may consider it appropriate to impose conditions which would have the effect of protecting trees, for example by requiring a building to be constructed within a specified "footprint" or, if landscaping is a reserved matter, by requiring the submission of details relating to trees to be retained on the site. Such details might include their location in relation to the proposed development and assessments of their health and stability. When granting full planning permission, conditions may be used, for example, to require the erection of protective fencing around trees during the course of development or restricting works which would adversely affect them. The LPA may consider it necessary in the circumstances to require erection of the fencing before the commencement of the development.

5.19   The LPA should decide in each case whether trees should be safeguarded by using a planning condition or TPO or both. In the Secretary of State's view, however, it is not reasonable to use conditions as a means of securing the long-term protection of trees when TPOs are available for this purpose.

Tree Planting

5.20   Planning conditions should be used, where appropriate, to secure the planting and establishment of new trees. Tree planting provides for the future amenity of a site and its surroundings, supplements existing tree cover or enhances areas where tree cover is sparse. The choice of species and location of planting will be influenced by the character and appearance of the area and the nature of the development, including the location of buildings, roads and underground services. The likely future growth of trees in relation to the development should be given due consideration. A condition may also provide for the protection of the planting area during development operations, maintenance of the trees during the first few years (the number of which should be specified) and the replacement of any trees which are removed or die within that time. A TPO may be used to protect trees which are planted pursuant to conditions.[60]

59   See in particular paragraph 48–52 and Annex A, paragraph 25–32 and 71–75.

60   See section 198(5) of the Act.

Landscaping

5.21 The LPA may wish to impose planning conditions to secure the landscaping of the development site. The design and implementation stages of landscaping may be addressed by separate conditions, occurring as they do at different stages. To ensure that a landscape scheme is prepared, conditions may require that no development should take place until the scheme for the site is approved, so long as this requirement is reasonable. Enforcing compliance with landscape schemes can pose problems, since work on them may not proceed until building operations are nearing completion. Where permission is granted for a substantial estate of houses, it may be appropriate to prohibit the erection of the last few houses until planting has been completed in accordance with the landscape scheme. In relation to permission for an industrial or office building, it would be possible to impose a condition prohibiting or restricting occupation of the building until such works have been completed.

PLANNING OBLIGATIONS

5.22 As well as being able to grant planning permission subject to conditions, the LPA may seek to enter into a planning obligation with a developer regarding the use or development of the land concerned.[61]

5.23 A planning obligation may:

(1) restrict the development or use of the land,

(2) require specified operations or activities to be carried out on the land,

(3) require the land to be used in a specified way, or

(4) require payments to be paid to the LPA as a single sum or periodically.

5.24 Guidance on planning obligations is in DOE Circular 1/97. Properly used, planning obligations can remedy genuine planning problems and enhance the quality of development. They can help reconcile the aims and interests of developers with the need to safeguard the local environment. For example, where a site includes woodland or open space which would be lost if a development proposal went ahead, the LPA may wish to seek agreement from the developer to provide some form of replacement facility on the site or on other land over which the developer has control. It may not be essential to provide an exact substitute: a woodland walkway, for example, may in some cases be an acceptable replacement for a green space. But there should be some relationship between what is lost and what is replaced, in scale as well as in kind. DETR welcomes the use of planning obligations by some developers in creating nature reserves, planting trees, establishing wildlife ponds and providing other nature conservation benefits.

61 Under section 106 of the Act (as substituted by section 12(1) of the Planning and Compensation Act 1991).

5.25 Section 106(1) of the Act enables the developer to enter into a planning obligation by making a unilateral undertaking as an alternative to doing so by agreement with the LPA. It is reasonable to expect LPAs and developers to try to resolve any planning objections to development proposals by agreement. But where developers consider that negotiations are being protracted unnecessarily or that unreasonable demands are being made, they may wish to enter into a planning obligation by unilateral undertaking. Unilateral undertakings, like other planning obligations, are usually drafted so that (1) they come into effect when planning permission is granted, and (2) there is no obligation to comply with them unless and until the developer implements the permission.

EFFECT OF PLANNING PERMISSION ON TPOs

5.26 Any cutting down or carrying out of work on protected trees which is required to implement a full planning permission does not require the consent of the LPA under the TPO (but see paragraph 6.14–6.16). When granting full planning permission the LPA should consider informing the applicant, by reference to the approved drawings, which trees they believe may be cut down or have work carried out on them without consent.

ENFORCEMENT

5.27 LPAs have an extensive and flexible range of enforcement powers to restrain or deal with breaches of planning control: enforcement notices, stop notices, planning contravention notices, breach of condition notices and provision for obtaining injunctions. Guidance on their use is given in Planning Policy Guidance Note 18, DOE Circular 10/97 and the Department's publication, *Enforcing Planning Control: A Good Practice Guide for Local Planning Authorities* (1997).

CHAPTER 6

Applications to carry out work on Protected Trees

No one I think is in my tree,
I mean it must be high or low;
That is you can't, you know, tune in
But it's alright,
That is I think it's not too bad.

– John Lennon, from *Strawberry Fields Forever*

EXEMPTIONS

6.1   There are a number of exemptions from the normal requirement to obtain the LPA's consent for cutting down or carrying out work on protected trees. Some are set out in the Act; others are found in the TPO.

EXEMPTIONS IN THE ACT

Dead, Dying and Dangerous Trees

6.2   The LPA's consent is not required for cutting down or carrying out work on trees which are dead or dying or have become dangerous.[62] In the Secretary of State's view, this exemption allows the removal of dead wood from a tree or the removal of dangerous branches from an otherwise sound tree. If a tree outside a woodland is removed under this exemption section 206 of the Act places the landowner under a duty to plant a replacement tree at the same place (for more guidance on the duty to replace trees see chapter 11 of this Guide).

6.3   A dead or dying tree may provide a habitat for plants and wildlife protected under the Wildlife and Countryside Act 1981. Trees with hollows or crevices, for example, provide important natural roost sites for many bat species covered by the 1981 Act. Anyone proposing to carry out work on a tree which is used as a roost for bats should first consult English Nature (see Annex 1).

6.4   Determining whether a tree is dead, dying or dangerous is not always a straightforward matter. Whether or not a tree has become dangerous for the purpose of the statutory exemption is a question of fact. In deciding whether trees have become dangerous the Courts adopt the sensible approach of a prudent citizen; there must be a present danger which need not be limited to disease or damage to the trees themselves. The threatened

---

62   See section 198(6)(a) of the Act. Under the felling licensing system (see section 9 of the Forestry Act 1967) the felling of "dying" trees is not exempt. But the felling of diseased trees is exempt where such work is necessary to prevent the spread of a quarantine pest or disease, and carried out in accordance with a notice served by a Plant Health Office of the Forestry Commission under the Plant Health (Forestry) (Great Britain) Order 1993, as amended.

danger does not actually have had to have occurred; it is sufficient to find that, by virtue of the state of the trees, their size, their position and such effect as any of those factors have, one can properly conclude that the trees have become dangerous. The Court will look at what is likely to happen, such as injury to a passing pedestrian.[63]

6.5　It is clear therefore that factors such as the size and position of a tree as well as its condition may be relevant, but the danger must be present. It does not mean that any individual who owns trees and wishes to remove them can say to himself, 'Having regard to their position, the way they have been planted and their unsuitability, I can see that in a number of years they are going to constitute a danger' and then cut them down. One has to look at the position at the time. If such damage is far off, remote and not immediate the trees do not come within the meaning of the exemption.

6.6　Anyone proposing to cut down a tree under this exemption is advised to give the LPA five days' notice before carrying out the work, except in an emergency. Anyone who is not sure whether the tree falls within the exemption is advised to obtain the advice of an arboriculturist.

6.7　If work is carried out on a protected tree under this exemption (or any of the other exemptions listed below), the burden of proof to show, on the balance of probabilities, that the tree was dead, dying or dangerous rests with the defendant.[64]

Statutory Obligations

6.8　The LPA's consent is not required for cutting down or carrying out work on trees in compliance with a statutory obligation.[65] For example, work carried out to remove or restrict the height of trees in accordance with a direction made by the Secretary of State under the Civil Aviation Act 1982[66] would be covered by this exemption.

Nuisance

6.9　The LPA's consent is not required for cutting down or carrying out work on trees so far as may be necessary to prevent or abate a nuisance.[67] The term "nuisance" is used in a legal sense, not its ordinary everyday sense.

6.10　Under common law[68] a landowner can cut the branches from a neighbour's trees if they overhang his or her property. The overhanging branches are regarded as a "nuisance" and may be cut at the boundary between the two properties whether or not they are causing any damage. The cut branches, including any fruit, remain the property of the neighbouring owner. The same rule applies to encroaching roots.[69] Two properties must be involved, and so householders cannot claim that the trees in their own garden are the cause of a nuisance to themselves.

63　See *Smith v Oliver* [1985] 2 PLR 1.

64　See *R v Alath Construction Ltd* (1991) EGLR 1.

65　See section 198(6)(b) of the Act.

66　See section 46; directions are intended to secure the safe and efficient use of land for civil aviation.

67　See section 198(6)(b) of the Act.

68　See *Lemmon v Webb* [1895] AC 1.

69　See *McCombe v Read* [1955] 2 All ER 458.

6.11 Whether the branches or roots of a *protected* tree can be cut back in this way under the exemption has not been settled by the Courts. In the unreported case of *Sun Timber Co. Ltd. v Leeds City Council* (a case involving overhanging branches) it was decided that the exemption applies only where the nuisance is "actionable", in other words where the overhanging branches are causing, or there is an immediate risk of their causing, actual foreseeable damage. If this interpretation of the exemption is correct the LPA's consent would be required under the TPO before cutting back branches or roots which are not causing damage.

Forestry Commission: Grant Schemes and Felling Licences

6.12 The LPA's consent is not required for cutting down trees in line with a plan of operations agreed by the Forestry Commission under one of their grant schemes,[70] or for the cutting down of trees in accordance with a felling licence.[71]

EXEMPTIONS IN THE TPO

6.13 A number of exemptions are also included in the TPO. The guidance below gives advice on the exemptions as they appear in the current model form of TPO in the 1999 Regulations. But reference should always be made to the particular provisions of the TPO in question before determining what work is exempt in any given case. For example, the exemptions conferred on statutory undertakers in TPOs made under previous Regulations are not in the same terms as those contained in TPOs made under the 1999 Regulations.

Planning Permission

6.14 The LPA's consent is not required for cutting down or carrying out work on trees if required to implement a full planning permission.[72] For example, the TPO is overridden if a tree has to be removed to make way for a new building for which full planning permission has been granted. In dealing with applications for planning permission LPAs consider a range of factors, including the potential loss of protected trees. Where, on balance, they decide to grant full planning permission protected trees may be cut down or cut back without any need to apply under the TPO, but only if such work is *required* to implement the planning permission.

6.15 The exemption is limited. If only outline planning permission has been granted, the LPA's consent under the TPO is still required before cutting down or carrying out work on protected trees.

6.16 The LPA's consent is also required before cutting down or carrying out work on trees to implement permitted development rights under the Town and Country Planning (General Permitted Development) Order 1995.[73] So anyone relying on permitted development rights to build an extension or put up a garden shed would have to obtain the LPA's consent if it was necessary in the process to cut down or carry out work on a protected tree.

70 See section 200(3) of the Act.

71 See section 198(6)(b) of the Act and section 15(6) of the Forestry Act 1967. But if a TPO is made *after* the FC have granted the felling licence, the LPA's additional consent for the felling *is* required.

72 See article 5(1)(d) of the 1999 Model Order.

73 Statutory Instruments 1995, No.418. Note that this general rule does not apply to specified activities carried out by statutory undertakers (see paragraph 6.21 of this Guide).

Fruit Trees

6.17 A fruit tree may be protected by a TPO provided, of course, the LPA believe it to be in the interests of amenity to do so.

6.18 If a fruit tree is protected by a TPO and cultivated in the course of a business, the LPA's consent is not required for cutting it down or carrying out work on it, as long as the tree work is in the interests of that business.[74]

6.19 If a fruit tree protected by a TPO is not cultivated on a commercial basis, it is necessary to obtain the LPA's consent before cutting it down. However, the LPA's consent is not needed before pruning any tree cultivated for the production of fruit, as long as the work is carried out in accordance with good horticultural practice.[75]

Statutory Undertakers and Other Bodies

6.20 Under the 1999 Model Order any of the following are treated as "statutory undertakers":

(1) railway, light railway, tramway, road transport, water transport, canal, inland navigation, dock, harbour, pier and lighthouse undertakers, and undertakings for the supply of hydraulic power;

(2) electricity operators,[76] public gas transporters, water and sewerage undertakers, telecommunications operators[77] and the Post Office;

(3) the Civil Aviation Authority or any body acting on their behalf.

6.21 Under the 1999 Model Order a statutory undertaker (or a contractor working at the undertaker's request) does not need to obtain the LPA's consent before cutting down or carrying out work on a tree which is situated on the undertaker's operational land[78] if necessary:

(1) in the interests of safety,

(2) when inspecting, repairing or renewing their mains, pipes, cables and other apparatus,

(3) when carrying out their permitted development rights under the Town and Country (General Permitted Development) Order 1995.

6.22 The Environment Agency do not need to obtain the LPA's consent before cutting down or carrying out work on trees to enable them to carry out their permitted development rights.[79] Similarly, drainage bodies do not need to obtain consent before cutting down or carrying out work on trees which interfere with their construction or maintenance works.[80]

---

74 See article 5(1)(b) of the 1999 Model Order.

75 See article 5(1)(c) of the 1999 Model Order. Note that TPOs made before the 1999 Regulations came into force provide an exemption in different terms, for the cutting down or carrying out of work on fruit trees which are "cultivated for fruit production growing or standing ... in an orchard or garden".

76 ie operators who hold a licence under section 6 of the Electricity Act 1989.

77 ie operators who hold a licence under section 7 of the Telecommunications Act 1984, to which the telecommunications code in that Act applies.

78 For the meaning of "operational land" see section 263 of the Act.

79 See article 5(1)(e) of the 1999 Model Order.

80 See article 5(1)(f) of the 1999 Model Order. For the definition of "drainage body" see the Land Drainage Act 1991.

Code of Practice for Utility Operators

6.23 Utility operators (ie gas, electricity, telecommunication (including cable communication) and water or sewerage undertakers) should take particular care to avoid damaging trees (and not just protected trees) when installing and maintaining their services above and below ground.

6.24 In 1995 the National Joint Utilities Group (NJUG) published guidelines on how this can be done.[81] All the utility operators are committed to implementing the guidelines. They emphasise the importance of regular contact between utility operators and the LPA, a point which is also made in DOE Circular 9/95 in relation to the carrying out of permitted development rights under the Town and Country (General Permitted Development) Order 1995. A code of practice for utility operators, which restates the principal messages in DOE Circular 9/95 and the NJUG guidelines, is at Annex 4.

Aerodromes

6.25 Certain civil and military aerodromes, selected on the basis of their importance to the national air transport system or their strategic importance, are officially "safeguarded" under the Town and Country Planning (Aerodromes and Technical Sites) Direction 1992. If the LPA propose to make a TPO on or near an aerodrome covered by the 1992 Direction, they should consult the Civil Aviation Authority (in the case of civil aerodromes) or the Ministry of Defence (in the case of military aerodromes). Advice on the 1992 Direction is given in DOE Circular 2/92.

Ancient Monuments

6.26 LPAs are not prevented from making TPOs on trees in the vicinity of scheduled ancient monuments, but before doing so they are advised to consult English Heritage (see Annex 1).

Churchyards

6.27 Trees in churchyards may be protected by a TPO, although such trees are not subject to felling control under the Forestry Act 1967.

FELLING LICENCES

6.28 Control over the felling of trees rests principally with the Forestry Commission who handle felling licence applications under section 9 of the Forestry Act 1967 (as amended). A licence is required under the 1967 Act for the felling of growing trees except in certain prescribed circumstances. The Forestry Commission investigate and may take legal action against anyone contravening the licensing laws.

6.29 If anyone proposes to fell trees which are protected by a TPO *and* the proposal also requires a felling licence under the 1967 Act, a felling licence application must first be put to the Forestry Commission (see Annex 1). The LPA have no power to grant or refuse any application under a TPO which should first have been put to the Commission; they can only deal with these applications if they are later referred to them by the Forestry Commission.[82] LPAs need to know therefore when the requirement to obtain a felling licence comes into play so that they know when to refer any would-be applicants under a TPO to the Forestry Commission.

81 Guidelines for the Planning, Installation and Maintenance of Utility Services in Proximity to Trees (NJUG 10).

82 See section 15 of the Forestry Act 1967.

Exemptions from Felling Control

6.30 A felling licence is required for the felling of a relatively low volume of wood (just five cubic metres can be felled in any calendar quarter without a licence, as long as no more than two cubic metres are sold), and so LPAs should be aware that a licence may be required for felling outside woodlands. Exemptions from the requirement to obtain a felling licence are set out in section 9 of the Forestry Act 1967 (as amended) and in Regulations made under that Act.[83] The main cases where a felling licence *is not* required, but where consent under a TPO is required, are for:

(1) the topping or lopping of trees,

(2) the felling of trees in gardens, orchards, churchyards or public open spaces,

(3) the felling of trees with a diameter of 8 centimetres or less (measured at 1.3 metres from the ground), or 15 centimetres in the case of coppice or underwood,

(4) the thinning of trees with a diameter of 10 centimetres or less.

If in doubt, ask the Forestry Commission.

Consultation between the Forestry Commission and LPA

6.31 The Forestry Commission will normally decide all felling licence applications involving trees protected by TPOs, after consulting the relevant LPA. If the Forestry Commission propose to grant a felling licence and the LPA disagree, the LPA may make a formal objection to the Commission. If the LPA make such an objection the application will be referred to the Secretary of State for the Environment, Transport and the Regions, who will decide the application under the TPO.[84]

6.32 Brief details of felling licence applications are kept on a public register, compiled by the Forestry Commission. Copies of the register, which also includes details of applications under the Woodland Grant Scheme, are sent to LPAs on a regular basis.[85] Although LPAs are consulted separately on any application involving a TPO,[86] they may wish to use the register as a means of providing an overview of applications in their area. If the LPA wish to be consulted on an application, or if they find an application involving a TPO on which they have not been consulted, they should contact their Regional Conservancy of the Forestry Commission.

TPO APPLICATIONS

Pre-Application

6.33 If a felling licence is not required an application for consent under the TPO must be made to the LPA. The applicant should consider seeking the advice of an arboriculturist or discussing the proposal informally with the LPA before making the application. The LPA will wish to visit the site at some stage before issuing a decision; giving them an opportunity to do so before an application is made may save time later on.

---

83 See The Forestry (Exceptions from Restriction of Felling) Regulations 1979 (SI 1979, No.792), as amended.

84 For the procedures involved see Schedule 3 of the Forestry Act 1967.

85 The register can also be seen on the Forestry Commission's website (www.forestry.gov.uk).

86 If protected trees are affected by the application the applicant is required to disclose details of the TPO.

6.34   Early discussion will give the LPA a chance to:

(1)   explain whether the work proposed is exempt from the need to apply for consent
      or requires an application to the Forestry Commission rather than the LPA,

(2)   advise on how best to present an application to the LPA,

(3)   guide the applicant generally about TPO procedures and the LPA's policies.

6.35   If a proposal is not discussed with the LPA before the application is made the applicant
       may be prepared to modify the application, or even withdraw it and submit a new one,
       after discussion with the LPA. But negotiations in this respect should not be long drawn
       out, and delay should never be used as a means of applying pressure on the applicant to
       agree to unwanted changes.

Who Can Apply?

6.36   Anyone can apply for consent under a TPO. You do not have to have a legal interest in the
       land and, unlike applications for planning permission, a TPO application does not have to
       be accompanied by a certificate that the applicant is the owner of the land concerned, or
       that the owner has been notified. For example, a person can apply to carry out work on
       trees which are situated in a neighbour's property. But an applicant who is not the owner of
       the trees is advised to consult the owner before making an application; the applicant is also
       advised to notify the owner as soon as the application has been submitted. It is legitimate
       for the LPA to ask applicants about their legal interests in the trees they propose to carry
       out work on. Their decision on the application should be based on the merits of the case,
       in the public interest. If they grant consent it will be for the applicant to make sure any
       necessary permission is obtained from the owner of the tree before carrying out the work.

The Application

6.37   An application under a TPO must:

(1)   be made in writing to the LPA,

(2)   state the reasons for making the application,

(3)   identify the trees to which the application relates, by reference to a plan if necessary,
      and

(4)   specify the operations for which consent is sought.

6.38   The LPA are likely to have their own application form. Although the applicant is under no
       obligation to use it, a standard form will help the LPA obtain the information they need in
       a consistent way. But the LPA have a responsibility here to keep their application form as
       simple as possible, without asking for unnecessary information. Whilst it is necessary for an
       application to identify the trees involved, it will not always be necessary to provide a plan
       for this purpose. The LPA are advised to ask the applicant to provide a simple sketch plan,
       and not a formal location plan, drawn to scale. The LPA should also avoid asking for
       multiple copies of the application, including the sketch plan. A model application form is
       at Annex 5.

6.39   It is vitally important that the application sets out clearly what work is proposed. This should be straightforward if the proposal is to fell a tree, as long as the tree is clearly identified. But if the proposal is to prune a tree the application should clarify exactly what work is envisaged. A proposal simply to "top" the tree or to "lop" or "cut back" some branches is too vague because it fails to describe the extent of the work. Applicants are advised not to submit their applications until they are in a position to present clear proposals. As suggested in paragraph 6.33 above they should consider first discussing their ideas with an arboriculturist or the tree officer of the LPA.

6.40   If the LPA receive a vague application they are advised to refer back to the applicant and seek clarification. If they grant consent to an application which is open to several interpretations the LPA may find it difficult to take enforcement action in cases where the work falls within one of those interpretations, even though the LPA believe the work exceeds that for which they intended to grant consent. Any clarification of an application should be confirmed in writing, either by modifying the original application or withdrawing it and submitting a new one.

6.41   Only one application is needed to carry out a number of different operations on the same tree (for example, to reduce some branches and lift the crown) or to carry out work on a number of trees (for example, to reduce the crowns of a line of trees). Similarly, a programme of work (such as specific operations which are to be repeated on an annual or regular basis, or a series of operations phased over a period of time) could be submitted as one application. Such applications are in fact encouraged as a means of promoting ongoing beneficial woodland management plans of, say, five years without the need for repeated applications over a relatively short period of time.

Acknowledging Receipt

6.42   The LPA will normally, as a matter of good administrative practice, acknowledge receipt of the application in writing, giving the name and telephone number of the LPA officer dealing with the case. The letter of acknowledgement should also briefly explain whether or not the LPA will be inviting comments on the application from local residents, authorities or groups, and whether the LPA intend to visit the site. Before acknowledging an application the LPA should check the trees are in fact protected by a TPO currently in force. A model acknowledgement letter is at Annex 6.

Publicity

6.43   The LPA are required to keep a register of all applications for consent which must be made available to the public at all reasonable hours.[87] The register should include details of every application under the TPO and the LPA's decision. They are not required to publicise applications more widely, for example by sending letters to local residents, putting up site notices or placing advertisements in local newspapers. However, where local people might be affected by the application or where there is likely to be a good deal of public interest, the LPA should consider displaying a site notice or notifying the residents, authorities or groups affected. In addition, where an application is submitted by a neighbour, the LPA should make sure the owner or occupier of the land on which the tree stands is informed and given a chance to comment.

---

87   See section 69 of the Act, as applied by the 1999 Model Order.

Considering Applications

6.44   If the LPA did not visit the site before the application was made they should do so at this stage. The site visit should be carried out by an officer with appropriate arboricultural knowledge and experience. If in the opinion of the LPA the work proposed is exempt (and as such does not require consent under the TPO) they should inform the applicant in writing as soon as possible. The LPA should not purport to "decide" the application by granting consent to the work; they should merely explain that the work does not require consent (and, where the felling of non-woodland trees is involved, explain the landowner's duty to plant a replacement tree: for more guidance on the duty to replace trees see chapter 11 of this Guide).

6.45   In considering applications the LPA are advised:

   (1)   to assess the amenity value of the tree or woodland and the likely impact of the proposal on the amenity of the area, and

   (2)   in the light of their assessment at (1) above, to consider whether or not the proposal is justified, having regard to the reasons put forward in support of it.

   They are advised also to consider whether any loss or damage is likely to arise if consent is refused or granted subject to conditions (see paragraph 14.7). In general terms, it follows that the higher the amenity value of the tree or woodland and the greater the impact of the application on the amenity of the area, the stronger the reasons needed before consent is granted. On the other hand, if the amenity value of the tree or woodland is low and the impact of the application in amenity terms is likely to be negligible, consent might be granted even if the LPA believe there is no particular arboricultural need for the work.

6.46   In deciding an application the LPA are not required to have regard to the development plan. Section 54A of the Act,[88] therefore, does not apply to the LPA's decision, which means that there is no general duty on the LPA to make their decision in accordance with the development plan (for more guidance on development plans see paragraph 5.2–5.4).

6.47   In dealing with an application in woodlands, the LPA must grant consent so far as accords with good forestry practice unless they are satisfied this would fail to secure the maintenance of the special character of the woodland or the woodland character of the area.[89] Where an application relates to trees in a conservation area the LPA are required to pay special attention to the desirability of preserving or enhancing the character or appearance of that area.[90]

---

88   As inserted by section 26 of the Planning and Compensation Act 1991: "Where, in making any determination under the planning Acts, regard is to be had to the development plan, the determination shall be made in accordance with the plan unless material considerations indicate otherwise".

89   See section 70(1A) of the Act, as applied by the 1999 Model Order.

90   See section 72 of the Planning (Listed Buildings and Conservation Areas) Act 1990.

DECISIONS

Powers

6.48   In dealing with an application the LPA may:

(1) refuse consent,

(2) grant consent unconditionally, or

(3) grant consent subject to such conditions as they think fit.[91]

Internal Procedures

6.49   The LPA may wish to distinguish between classes of applications which may be decided by officers of the Council under delegated powers (for example, minor pruning work which raises no objections) and those to be decided by a committee or sub-committee (for example, a proposal to cut down trees which is opposed by local residents).

Granting Consent

6.50   The LPA must decide the application before them; they should not issue a decision which substantially alters the work applied for. The LPA could, however, grant consent for less work than that applied for (for example, by allowing the reduction of the crown of a tree by 20% rather than the 50% applied for), although the applicant would retain a right of appeal against that part of the application which was effectively refused.

6.51   Where an application relates to a number of different operations on one or more trees the LPA may refuse consent for some of the operations and grant consent for others. Their decision notice should, of course, make absolutely clear what is being authorised.

Granting Consent Subject to Conditions

6.52   The legislation does not place restrictions on the LPA's power to impose conditions on a consent. But this does not mean the power is unlimited. In the Secretary of State's view conditions should always relate to the authorised work and be fair and reasonable in the circumstances of each case. In deciding whether or not a condition would be fair and reasonable in the circumstances the LPA should consider whether there is a definite need for it. Would the condition help tackle a specific problem? The argument that it would do no harm would not itself be sufficient justification for imposing it.

6.53   Conditions should be precisely worded so that the applicant is left in no doubt about its interpretation and the LPA are satisfied it can be enforced. Where several trees are to be replaced it may not be good enough, for example, to require a replanting scheme to be submitted for the LPA's approval. In such a case consent should be granted on condition that the trees *are planted* in accordance with a replanting scheme to be submitted for the LPA's approval (for further advice on conditions which leave detailed matters open for later discussion, see paragraph 6.56 below).

6.54   LPAs should bear in mind that they are liable to pay compensation to any person who suffers loss or damage as a result of a grant of consent subject to conditions. In *Deane v Bromley Borough Council*,[92] for example, consent was granted to prune 26 trees subject to a condition that the work was carried out by an approved contractor. The Lands Tribunal

---

91   See section 70(1) of the 1990 Act, as applied by the 1999 Model Order.

92   (1992) J.P.L. 279.

accepted that the applicant could have carried out the work himself and awarded compensation based on the difference between the total cost of the contracted work and the costs he would have incurred by hiring equipment.

6.55   Conditions are commonly used to secure the planting of replacement trees, to impose a time limit on the duration of consent and to regulate the standard of the authorised work.

Replacement Trees

6.56   Prior discussion with the applicant should help the LPA formulate, at the time of consent, a mutually acceptable condition that makes clear the size, species and location of the replacement tree and the period within which it is to be planted. In cases where there has been no discussion, and where the applicant has given the LPA no indication of any replanting proposals, the LPA may still frame a condition that might be discharged without any further ado. For example, a condition may require the planting of a tree of W size and X species, at Y location and within Z period of time *or such other size, species, location or period as may be agreed in writing by the LPA.* Whilst the LPA can enforce this condition the door is left open for further discussion about the details if wanted. But the applicant could, if content, go ahead and plant the tree without any further discussion with the LPA. LPAs are therefore advised to avoid conditions which have the effect *always* of requiring further discussion (ie by requiring the planting of a replacement of a size, species etc to be agreed in writing with the LPA). LPAs should also note that a condition does not have to require the replacement tree to be planted in exactly the same place as the original. It may not be necessary, therefore, to impose a condition requiring the removal of the original tree's stump.

6.57   The LPA may enforce this type of condition by serving on the landowner a tree replacement notice (for more advice on these notices see chapter 11 of this Guide). Tree replacement notices cannot be used, though, to enforce the maintenance of newly planted trees, so LPAs are advised not to impose maintenance requirements in their conditions. But they may impose a condition to ensure that further replacements are planted if any newly planted trees die.[93] A condition of this kind may also meet concerns that many replacement trees planted in compliance with a condition are not automatically protected by the original TPO (see paragraph 11.15).

Duration of consent

6.58   The LPA may in some cases believe it appropriate to impose a time limit (of, say, two years) on the duration of the consent. After the expiry of the time limit a further application for consent would have to be made.

Standard of work

6.59   The LPA may wish to use their powers to ensure that tree work or planting is carried out in accordance with good arboricultural practice. This may be done, where appropriate, by imposing a condition requiring compliance with the relevant current British Standard.[94] The LPA should not, however, use such conditions without first considering whether they are relevant and reasonable in the particular circumstances of each case.

93 For example: "If, within a period of two years from the date of planting, the tree (or any other tree planted in replacement for it) is removed, uprooted or destroyed or dies, another tree of the same size and species shall be planted at the same place, or in accordance with any variation for which the local planning authority give their written consent."

94 The principal British Standards currently in force are: BS 3998:1989, Recommendations for Tree Work (which is particularly relevant for pruning works); BS 4428:1989, Code of Practice for General Landscape Operations, BS 4043:1989, Transplanting Root-balled Trees and BS 3936:1992, Part 1: Nursery Stock – Specification for Trees and Shrubs, which may in some circumstances be relevant for the planting of replacement trees.

6.60 Advice on the use of conditions when granting planning permission, including conditions on landscaping and the protection and planting of trees, is given in DOE Circular 11/95.

Refusing Consent

6.61 When the LPA decide to refuse consent (or grant consent subject to conditions) they should:

(1) give their reasons for the decision. These should relate to each of the applicant's reasons for making the application. For example, if a person applies for consent to cut down a tree on the grounds that (i) it is causing damage to his property, (ii) it blocks out too much light from his property, and (iii) it has little "amenity value", the refusal notice should address each of these points. It would not be sufficient simply to refuse such an application "because the work proposed would be detrimental to amenity",[95]

(2) explain the applicant's right of appeal to the Secretary of State against the decision,

(3) explain the applicant's right to compensation for loss or damage suffered as a result of the LPA's decision (this will depend on whether or not the LPA have decided to issue a certificate under article 5 of a TPO made before 2 August 1999),[96] and how a claim should be made.

A model refusal notice is at Annex 7.

Advice

6.62 The LPA may wish to attach to their decision notice advice on certain aspects of the decision. Useful advice (sometimes known as an "informative") can be given, for example, on how best to plant a replacement tree or how to carry out work in accordance with good practice. An applicant who does not own a tree might be advised to notify and, if necessary, obtain the permission of, the owner before carrying out any work for which consent has been granted. The owner's permission would be needed, for example, if the consent would involve the applicant (who may be a neighbour) carrying out work to the tree on the owner's side of the boundary. TPO consents do not override the need to obtain any such private permission that may be required from time to time.

6.63 The LPA could also give advice on where people can obtain specialist advice. General advice is available from the Arboricultural Association or the Arboricultural Advisory and Information Service or, in respect of woodlands, the Forestry Commission or Institute of Chartered Foresters (see Annex 1). When granting consent the LPA may wish to consider providing the applicant with a copy of their decision notice which can be passed on to the contractor who carries out the tree work.

Article 5 Certificates

6.64 When refusing consent or granting consent subject to conditions under a TPO which was made before 2 August 1999 the LPA may issue, in relation to any tree to which the refusal of consent (or conditions) relate, a certificate under article 5 of that TPO

---

95 Where the LPA grant consent subject to conditions, they should give their reasons for each condition imposed.

96 But note that an article 5 certificate cannot be issued if the application is under a TPO that was made on or after 2 August 1999 (see paragraph 6.64).

(an "article 5 certificate").[97] TPOs made on or after 2 August 1999, which have to follow the model form of TPO included in the 1999 Regulations, make no provision for these certificates. So in dealing with applications for consent under these TPOs LPAs cannot issue article 5 certificates.

6.65 An article 5 certificate may be issued if the LPA are satisfied:

(1) that their decision is in the interests of good forestry, or

(2) that the trees, groups of trees or woodlands to which the certificate relates have an "outstanding" or "special" amenity value.

In simple terms the effect of an article 5 certificate is to remove the LPA's liability under the TPO to pay compensation for loss or damage caused or incurred as a result of their decision.

6.66 LPAs should note that an article 5 certificate cannot be issued where an application for a felling licence in respect of a group of trees or woodlands has been referred to the LPA by the Forestry Authority under section 15 of the Forestry Act 1967.

6.67 LPAs are advised to use article 5 certificates with discretion and not simply as a means of avoiding the potential liability of compensation. The LPA should consider each case on its merits and must, when issuing a certificate, be satisfied that their decision is in the interests of good forestry, or that the trees, groups of trees or woodlands have an "outstanding" or a "special" amenity value.

Good Forestry

6.68 Before issuing a certificate that that their decision is in the interests of good forestry the LPA are advised to satisfy themselves that there is a "forestry context" to justify it. In the Secretary of State's view it is unlikely to be appropriate to issue a "good forestry" certificate in cases where there is no such context but where the LPA believe their decision is in the interests of "good arboriculture".

Special or outstanding amenity value

6.69 Before issuing a "special" or "outstanding" certificate the LPA should consider carefully the amenity value of the trees and whether that value amounts to something that could reasonably be described as "special" or "outstanding", using the ordinary meanings of the words. The words should not be treated as if they have the same meaning. The LPA may in some cases consider that the trees have both a "special" and an "outstanding" amenity value, but in most cases they would normally be expected to choose just one of these terms. For example, the term "outstanding" may be used in relation to dominant features of the landscape, whereas the term "special" may be attributed to trees that perform a specific function in their setting, such as screening development operations.

6.70 Each appeal against a "special" or "outstanding" certificate is treated by the Secretary of State on its merits, having regard to all the representations submitted to him. But in general terms the Secretary of State draws a distinction between trees which merit a TPO in the interests of amenity and trees which merit a certificate of special or outstanding amenity value. In deciding whether to uphold a certificate the Secretary of State will consider whether or not there are "special" or "outstanding" factors that distinguish the trees from other *protected trees*, rather than trees generally.

97 Assuming the TPO follows the form of the Model Order included in the Town and Country Planning (Tree Preservation Order) Regulations 1969.

Good Practice

6.71 As a matter of good practice the LPA should:

(1) leave the applicant in no doubt that a certificate has actually been issued. For example, a decision simply refusing consent *on the grounds* that the trees have a special amenity value is vague; the LPA should *certify* that they are satisfied the trees have a special amenity value,

(2) explain their reasons for issuing the certificate. The LPA should state why they believe a tree has an "outstanding" or "special" amenity value, or why they believe their decision is in the interests of good forestry,

(3) explain the effect of the certificate (ie that it removes the LPA's liability under the TPO to pay compensation for loss or damage caused or incurred in consequence of the decision), and

(4) explain the applicant's right of appeal to the Secretary of State against the certificate.

A model article 5 certificate is at Annex 8.

Replanting Directions

6.72 The 1999 Model Order includes special provisions about the replanting of woodlands which are felled in the course of forestry operations. Most applications involving forestry operations require a felling licence and are therefore handled by the Forestry Commission (see paragraph 6.28–6.32). But the LPA will from time to time deal with applications which do not require a felling licence (such as applications to fell coppice with a diameter of no more than 15 centimetres). In such cases, the LPA are required to grant consent to woodland applications in accordance with the principles of good forestry (unless the consent would fail to secure the special character of the woodland or the woodland character of the area).[98] If the LPA grant consent, they may give the landowner a direction (not a condition) to replant the land (a "replanting direction"). They may wish to consult the Forestry Commission on the details of the replanting direction.

6.73 A replanting direction must be in writing and must specify the time within which the replanting should be completed. It may also include requirements relating to:

(1) the species and numbers of trees per hectare;

(2) the preparation of the land prior to replanting; and

(3) the erection of fencing necessary for the protection of the newly planted trees.[99]

6.74 When giving a replanting direction, the LPA should explain that an appeal against it may be made to the Secretary of State.

6.75 Although compensation is not payable under the TPO for losses incurred as a result of complying with a replanting direction, the LPA are liable to pay compensation in certain circumstances (see paragraph 14.9–14.11).

98 See section 70(1A) of the Act, as applied to the 1999 Model Order.

99 See article 8(3) of the 1999 Model Order.

LOCAL AUTHORITY APPLICATIONS

6.76   LPAs are no longer required to apply to the Secretary of State if they want consent to cut down or carry out work on trees or woodlands protected by TPOs.[100] They are now responsible for determining their own applications (ie applications made by any department of the Council as a whole and not just their planning department).

Publicising Applications

6.77   Before determining their own application the LPA must publicise it by displaying a site notice on or near the land in question for at least 21 days. The purpose of the notice is to inform local people about the proposal and give them an opportunity to submit their comments on it. The site notice must:

(1)   give details about the nature of the application (identifying the trees, the work proposed and the LPA's reasons for the application), including an address where a copy can be inspected,

(2)   give an address to which any comments about the application should be sent,

(3)   give a date by which representations have to be made. At least 21 days from the date of display of the site notice must be given.

Deciding Applications

6.78   The application must not be decided by a committee or sub-committee of the Council which is responsible (wholly or partly) for managing the land to which the application relates. Nor can the application be decided by an officer of the Council whose responsibilities relate in any way to the management of the land. (It is for the LPA to decide their own internal arrangements in the light of this requirement; they have for many years been subject to similar restrictions in relation to the handling of their own applications to develop land.[101]) Before reaching their decision the LPA must take into account any representations made by the date given in the site notice; and they must give notice of their decision to all people who made representations.

100   See regulation 17 of the 1999 Regulations (which amends the Town and Country Planning General Regulations 1992, Statutory Instruments 1992, No.1492).

101   Under the Town and Country Planning General Regulations 1992 (SI 1992, No.1492). See also DOE Circular 19/92.

CHAPTER 7

Appeals Against Local Planning Authority Decisions

"Wild Nature, a heathscape," said the painter, handing K the picture. It showed two stunted trees standing far apart from each other in darkish grass. In the background was a many-hued sunset. "Fine," said K. "I'll buy it." "Here's the companion picture," said the painter. It might have been intended as a companion picture, but there was not the slightest difference that one could see between it and the other: here were the two trees, here the grass, and there the sunset. "I'll buy both of them and hang them up in my office." "You seem to like the subject," said the painter fishing out a third canvas. "I'll take that one as well," said K. "How much for the three pictures?" "We'll settle that next time," said the painter. "You're in a hurry. Some people won't have anything to do with these subjects because they're too depressing, but there are always people like yourself who prefer depressing pictures."

– Franz Kafka, *The Trial*

THE RIGHT OF APPEAL

7.1   Each TPO sets out when an appeal to the Secretary of State can be made following an application for consent to cut down or carry out work on a protected tree.

7.2   An appeal may be brought against any of the following:

(1)   the LPA's refusal of consent;

(2)   any condition attached to the LPA's consent;

(3)   any article 5 certificate (see paragraph 6.64–6.71) issued by the LPA on refusing consent or granting consent subject to conditions;

(4)   any replanting direction (see paragraph 6.72–6.75) issued by the LPA on granting consent to fell any part of a woodland; or

(5)   the LPA's failure to notify the applicant of their decision within two months or 8 weeks[102] from the date they received the application (or such extended period as may be agreed by the applicant and LPA in writing). Once an appeal has been made, the LPA cannot decide the application, which is treated as though it had been refused by the LPA. The appeal may be withdrawn, though, if it becomes clear that the LPA would be prepared to grant consent.

---

102 Refer to the TPO in question: some give a period of two months, others give a period of 8 weeks.

TPOs made on or after 2 August 1999 include an extra ground of appeal against:

(6) the LPA's refusal to agree a matter that required their agreement under the terms of a condition of consent. For example, say the LPA grant consent to the cutting down of a tree subject to a condition that a replacement tree is planted of a size and species, and in a location to be agreed with the LPA. If the LPA and applicant subsequently fail to agree any of these matters the applicant may appeal to the Secretary of State.

7.3 Note also that TPOs made on or after 2 August 1999 make no provision for article 5 certificates (see paragraph 6.64). In dealing with an application for consent under such a TPO the LPA will not be able to issue a certificate, and so no appeal under sub-paragraph (3) above will arise. But appeals against article 5 certificates will continue to arise, of course, in relation to TPOs made before 2 August 1999.

7.4 Guidance on appeals against tree replacement notices, which are served by LPAs under section 207 of the Act, is given in chapter 12 of this Guide.

HOW TO APPEAL

7.5 An appeal can only be made by the applicant (or an agent acting on the applicant's behalf). The appeal must be made in writing within 28 days of receiving the LPA's decision, certificate or direction, though the Secretary of State may allow a longer period. There is no charge but appeals are expensive for the Government to administer and time-consuming for all concerned. The parties should not rule out further discussions after the appeal has been made; difficulties or misunderstandings can sometimes be resolved even at this stage, leading to the eventual withdrawal of the appeal and a saving of public resources.

PROCEDURE

7.6 Appeals are handled in the first instance by the relevant Government Office for the Region (see Annex 1). Either party may if they wish have the appeal dealt with at a hearing or public local inquiry, but in practice most cases are dealt with by an exchange of written statements followed by a site visit (the "written representations procedure").

Written Representations

7.7 The written representations procedure is a quicker, simpler and cheaper alternative to the hearing/public inquiry method. Under the 1999 Regulations written representations now have to be submitted within set time limits.[103] The Government Office ask the appellant to complete an appeal form, including the grounds of appeal. The Government Office then write to the LPA, enclosing an appeal questionnaire. The date of this letter usually marks the formal starting date of the appeal. The LPA are required to submit the completed questionnaire, together with background papers relevant to the appeal, to the Government Office within two weeks of the starting date. Copies of these papers, including the questionnaire, should be sent to the appellant at the same time. If the parties wish to submit additional representations they must do so within six weeks of the starting date.

103 See regulations 11 to 16.

The LPA's Statement

7.8   The LPA are advised to invite any third parties who commented on the original application to submit representations on the appeal. These representations should be sent by third parties directly to the Government Office. The LPA should involve third parties at an early stage so that they are given sufficient time to submit their representations within six weeks of the starting date.

7.9   LPAs are not required to submit their additional representations in any particular form. They must themselves judge what sort of submission they wish to put forward, but they are advised to concentrate on the main controversial issues raised by the appeal. Many appeal statements are unnecessarily long, containing material which is not relevant. Background documents submitted with the appeal questionnaire may often be sufficient to present the LPA's case. Additional information should be presented as concisely as possible. For example, in deciding an appeal the Secretary of State is not required under section 54A of the Act to have regard to the development plan, and so his decision does not have to be made in accordance with that plan. In the Secretary of State's view, therefore, it is not necessary for the LPA to include detailed representations about the tree policies in their development plan. Similarly, whilst the LPA may consider it relevant to mention that the appeal tree has been the subject of a number of applications by the appellant in the past, a detailed history of those applications is unlikely to be necessary. A model format for LPA statements is at Annex 9.

7.10   The Government Office send a copy of the LPA's representations to the appellant. Any third party representations submitted within six weeks of the starting date are sent to both parties. The parties are given a further two weeks to provide any final representations on any new matters arising. Late and repetitious representations are discouraged. Whether intended to reinforce points already made, have the last word, or save the best arguments to the end, such tactics confer no advantage and only prolong the appeal process.

Site Visit

7.11   After the exchange of written representations the Government Office arrange for an officer of the Department or an arboriculturist appointed by the Department to visit the appeal site. The inspecting officer is responsible for producing an independent and impartial report on the main issues raised under the appeal, which will help the Secretary of State reach a decision on the case.

7.12   The inspecting officer is usually accompanied by representatives of both parties to the appeal. The presence of the appellant may be required to gain access to the site, identify the appeal trees or clarify the work for which consent is sought. No discussion about the merits of the appeal is allowed, although the inspecting officer may ask questions on factual matters.

7.13   Arranging accompanied site visits can delay the handling of appeals. Unaccompanied site visits may be arranged with the consent of both parties, provided the inspecting officer can gain access to the site and has sufficient information to assess all aspects of the case.

Hearings and Public Local Inquiries

7.14   If either party exercise their right to a hearing or public local inquiry, the Government Office liaise with the Planning Inspectorate, and an inspector is appointed to hear the case and submit a report to the Secretary of State.

The Secretary of State's Decision

7.15   The Secretary of State may allow or dismiss the appeal. He may reverse or vary any part of the LPA's decision, cancel any article 5 certificate or cancel or vary any replanting direction. He may deal with the application as if it had been made to him in the first instance. He may allow an appeal in part. The decision notice is sent to the appellant and copied to the LPA. A copy will also be sent, on request, to any third party who submitted representations. The LPA should, when they receive an appeal decision, record the outcome on the public register which they are required to keep (see paragraph 6.43).

7.16   The Secretary of State's decision is made in the light of the inspecting officer's report and the representations submitted by the parties. In dealing with appeals against the LPA's refusal of an application for consent, the Secretary of State's policy is to consider the amenity value of the appeal tree or trees, how this value would be affected by the proposed work, and the reasons given for the application. The Secretary of State's general approach in dealing with appeals against "special" or "outstanding" article 5 certificates is described in paragraph 6.70.

COSTS

7.17   The parties must meet their own expenses if an appeal is dealt with under the written representations procedure. In the case of appeals dealt with by hearing or inquiry, an application for an award of costs may be made by one party on the grounds of the other party's "unreasonable behaviour" which causes unnecessary expense. An application should be made to the inspector at the hearing or inquiry who will make a recommendation to the Secretary of State. If a hearing or inquiry is cancelled as a result of one party's withdrawal any application for an award of costs should be submitted to the relevant Government Office for the Region. All applications for costs are decided by the Secretary of State.[104]

HIGH COURT CHALLENGE

7.18   The validity of the Secretary of State's decision on an appeal cannot be challenged in any legal proceedings *except* by way of application to the High Court.[105] If either the appellant or LPA wish to make a challenge the procedure is the same as that for challenging the validity of a TPO (see paragraph 3.45–3.47). An application to the High Court may be made on the grounds:

(1)   that the Secretary of State's decision is not within the powers of the Act; or

(2)   that the requirements of the Act or the TPO have not been complied with in relation to that decision.

104   For more details, see DOE Circular 8/93. A pamphlet *Cost Awards in Planning Appeals – A Guide for Appellants* can be obtained from the Planning Inspectorate, 10/28 Tollgate House, Houlton Street, Bristol, BS2 9DJ (telephone: 0117 987 8594).

105   See section 284 and 288 of the Act.

7.19   The High Court may suspend the operation of the Secretary of State's decision until the final determination of the proceedings. The Court may also quash the decision if satisfied that it is not within the powers of the Act or that the interests of the applicant have been substantially prejudiced by a failure to comply with the requirements of the Act or TPO.

CHAPTER 8

Modifying and Revoking Consents

The flowers left thick at nightfall in the wood
This Eastertide call into mind the men,
Now far from home, who, with their sweethearts, should
Have gathered them and will do never again.

– Edward Thomas, *In Memorium (Easter, 1915)*

ORDERS MODIFYING OR REVOKING A CONSENT

8.1 Any consent granted under a TPO enures for the benefit of the land, unless the consent states otherwise.[106] In other words a consent attaches to the land rather than to the applicant personally. So, unless it says otherwise, an unused consent granted on an application made by a previous owner of the land could be used by the current landowner.

8.2 TPOs made before 2 August 1999 include provisions which enable the LPA to modify or revoke any consent granted under the TPO.[107]

8.3 The LPA can modify or revoke a consent:

(1) by referring the revocation or modification order to the Secretary of State for confirmation; or

(2) by dealing with the matter themselves without reference to the Secretary of State. The LPA can choose this option only where all parties affected by the order have first notified the LPA that they have no objections to the proposed order.

Either way a revocation or modification order does not affect any work already carried out in accordance with the consent.

OPPOSED CASES: ORDERS CONFIRMED BY THE SECRETARY OF STATE

8.4 Under this procedure the LPA make an order revoking or modifying a consent and submit it to the relevant Government Office for the Region (see Annex 1) together with a statement of their reasons for making the order. They must also send a copy of the order and statement to the owner and occupier of the land affected, and anyone else who in their opinion will be affected by the order. They should also point out that no further work may be carried out

---

106 Unless, for example, the consent is granted subject to a condition that the approved work is carried out within a specific period. See section 75 of the Act, as applied by the 1999 Model Order.

107 These provisions are not included in TPOs made on or after 2 August 1999.

under the consent until the Secretary of State has decided whether or not to confirm the revocation or modification order. Anyone served with a copy of the order who wishes to oppose it may ask for an opportunity to appear before a hearing, but must do so within 28 days from the service of the notice. If both sides agree (ie the person opposing the order and the LPA) the Secretary of State may decide not to set up a hearing, but decide the matter in the light of representations submitted to him in writing.

UNOPPOSED CASES: ORDERS BROUGHT INTO EFFECT BY THE LPA

8.5   This procedure applies only where the owner and occupier of the land and other people affected by the revocation or modification order inform the LPA in writing that they have no objections to the proposed order. Even so, on making the order the LPA must put an advertisement in a local newspaper explaining that the order has been made, and the advertisement must specify:

(1) a period (which must be no less than 28 days from the date of the advertisement's appearance in the newspaper) within which anyone affected by the order may, by writing to the relevant Government Office, ask for an opportunity to appear before a hearing in respect of the order, and

(2) the period (which must be no less than 14 days from the period referred to in sub-paragraph (1) above) at the end of which the order will take effect if no-one writes to the Government Office.

8.6   The LPA must write to the owner, occupier and other people affected by the revocation or modification order, providing the same details as those given in the advertisement. They must also send a copy of the advertisement to the Government Office within three days of its publication.

8.7   The forms of advertisement and notice which LPAs are required to follow when modifying or revoking *planning permissions* are prescribed in the Town and Country Planning General Regulations 1992.[108] LPAs are not required to follow these forms when revoking or modifying a *consent under a TPO*, but they may find them useful.

8.8   If no-one affected by the order writes to the Government Office and the Secretary of State does not direct the LPA to refer the order to him for confirmation, the order takes effect on the date specified in the advertisement.

---

108 See regulation 17 and Schedule 3, Statutory Instruments 1992, No.1492.

CHAPTER 9

Trees in Conservation Areas

They will come again, the leaf and the flower, to arise
From squalor of rottenness into the old splendour,
And magical scents to a wondering memory bring;
The same glory, to shine upon different eyes.
Earth cares for her own ruins, naught for ours.
Nothing is certain, only the certain spring.

– Laurence Binyon, from *The Burning of the Leaves*

CONSERVATION AREAS

9.1   The law relating to conservation areas is in Part II of the Planning (Listed Buildings and Conservation Areas) Act 1990. Conservation areas are areas of special architectural or historical interest the character or appearance of which it is desirable to preserve or enhance. They are designated by LPAs and are often, though not always, centred around listed buildings. Other buildings and landscape features, including trees, may also contribute to the special character of a conservation area.

TREES IN CONSERVATION AREAS: SECTION 211 NOTICES

9.2   Trees in conservation areas which are already protected by a TPO are subject to the normal TPO controls. But the Town and Country Planning Act 1990 also makes special provision for trees in conservation areas which are not the subject of a TPO. Under section 211 anyone proposing to cut down or carry out work on a tree in a conservation area is required to give the LPA six weeks' prior notice (a "section 211 notice"). The purpose of this requirement is to give the LPA an opportunity to consider whether a TPO should be made in respect of the tree.

EXEMPTIONS

9.3   Exemptions from the requirement to give a section 211 notice are set out in the 1999 Regulations.[109] You do not have to give the LPA six weeks' notice:

(1)   for cutting down trees in accordance with a felling licence granted by the Forestry Commission or a plan of operations approved by the Commission under one of their grant schemes,

(2)   for work which is exempt from the requirement to apply for consent under a TPO (for more details see chapter 6 of this Guide),[110]

---

109 See regulation 10.

110 Anyone proposing to cut down a tree in a conservation area on the grounds that it is dead, dying or has become dangerous is advised to give the LPA five days' notice before carrying out the work, except in an emergency.

(3) for work carried out by, or on behalf of, the LPA (ie the Council as a whole and not just its planning department),

(4) for work on a tree with a diameter not exceeding 75 millimetres (or 100 millimetres if cutting down trees to improve the growth of other trees, ie thinning operations).[111]

GIVING NOTICE

9.4 A section 211 notice does not have to be in any particular form. But it must describe the work proposed and include sufficient particulars to identify the trees. It may be helpful to use the standard "notification form" provided by the LPA, although they cannot insist on its use.

9.5 It is vitally important that the section 211 notice sets out clearly what work is proposed. This should be straightforward if the proposal is to fell a tree, as long as the tree is clearly identified. But if the proposal is to prune a tree the section 211 notice should clarify exactly what work is envisaged. A proposal simply to "top" the tree or to "lop" or "cut back" some branches is too vague because it fails to describe the extent of the work. People are advised not to submit a section 211 notice until they are in a position to present a clear proposal. They should consider first discussing their ideas with an arboriculturist or the tree officer of the LPA.

9.6 If the LPA receive a vague section 211 notice they are advised to refer back to the person who submitted it. Any clarification of the proposal should be confirmed in writing, either by modifying the original section 211 notice or withdrawing it and submitting a new one.

WHAT THE LPA CAN DO

9.7 The LPA can deal with a section 211 notice in one of three ways. They may:

(1) make a TPO if justified in the interests of amenity. The proposal would then have to be the subject of a formal application under the TPO,[112] or

(2) decide not to make a TPO and allow the six week period to expire, at which point the proposed work may go ahead as long as it is carried out within two years from the date of the notice, or

(3) decide not to make a TPO and inform the applicant that the work can go ahead.

The LPA cannot refuse consent. Nor can they grant consent subject to conditions (such as a condition requiring the planting of a replacement tree). This is because a section 211 notice is not, and should not be treated as, an application for consent under a TPO.

---

111 Diameter as measured at 1.5m above ground level. In the case of multi-stemmed trees, the exemption applies only if the diameters of all the stems are less than 75 millimetres or 100 millimetres, as the case may be.

112 It is clearly desirable for the LPA to ensure that they make the TPO within the 6 week period, though they are not precluded from doing so afterwards (see *R v North Hertfordshire District Council, ex parte Hyde* [1989] 3 PLR 89).

ACKNOWLEDGING RECEIPT

9.8   The LPA should consider whether the proposed work is exempt from the requirement to give a section 211 notice or requires a felling licence. In either case the person who gave the notice should be informed as soon as possible. Otherwise the LPA are advised to acknowledge receipt of the section 211 notice in writing. The letter should explain that the proposal can proceed at the end of the six week period unless a TPO is made. The six week period starts from the date of the section 211 notice[113] and the letter should specify the date marking the end of the period. The letter should also explain whether the LPA will publicise the notice giving local residents, authorities and groups an opportunity to comment on the proposal. A model acknowledgement letter is at Annex 10.

PUBLICITY

9.9   Although the LPA are not required to publicise a section 211 notice they are advised to consider seeking the views of local residents, authorities or groups, particularly in cases where there is likely to be public interest. There are likely to be cases where the LPA consider no publicity is warranted. In cases where they believe some publicity is warranted, the LPA should decide what form it should take having regard to the particular circumstances of the case. They may decide to invite views on the proposal, for example, by writing to nearby residents and groups or by displaying a site notice or even by placing an advertisement in a local newspaper. If the LPA decide to publicise the proposal they should, of course, take into account any comments duly submitted before deciding whether or not to intervene by making a TPO.

PUBLIC REGISTER

9.10   Quite apart from any publicity which the LPA may consider appropriate, they are required to keep available for public inspection a register of all section 211 notices.[114] The Secretary of State has determined that the register should include the following particulars:

(1)   the address of the land on which the tree stands and sufficient information to identify the tree and the work proposed;

(2)   the date of the section 211 notice and who served it;

(3)   the decision of the LPA (if they make one) and the date of the decision; and

(4)   an index for tracing entries.

---

113   See section 211(3)(b)(ii) of the Act.

114   See section 214 of the Act.

CONSIDERATION OF SECTION 211 NOTICES

Site Visit: Does the Tree Merit a TPO?

9.11   The LPA's main consideration should be whether the tree merits a TPO. The LPA should therefore assess the amenity value of the tree. Special attention must be paid to the desirability of preserving the character or appearance of the conservation area.[115] Responses to any publicity should also be considered. If the LPA decide that the tree does not merit a TPO they should either allow the six week period to expire or write to the person who gave the section 211 notice to say the work may go ahead. They may wish to offer practical advice on how the work should be carried out, *but they cannot impose conditions.*

Would it be Expedient to Make a TPO?

9.12   If the tree merits a TPO the LPA may yet decide that it would not be expedient to make one. The proposed work, for example, may be in line with good practice. If a TPO is made, in addition to fulfilling the usual statutory requirements (sending out a copy of the TPO, giving notice that objections may be made etc: see chapter 3 of this Guide), the LPA should explain to the person who gave the section 211 notice that an application for consent under the TPO may be made at any time. At this stage, the LPA may also be in a position to indicate what work (if any) they would be prepared to allow and whether or not any conditions would be imposed.

PENALTIES

9.13   Anyone who cuts down, uproots, tops, lops, wilfully destroys or wilfully damages a tree in a conservation area without giving a section 211 notice (or otherwise in contravention of section 211) is guilty of an offence. The same penalties as those for contravening a TPO apply (see chapter 10 of this Guide). For example, anyone who cuts down a tree in a conservation area without giving a section 211 notice is liable, if convicted in the Magistrates' Court, to a fine of up to £20,000. Anyone who carries out work in a way that is not likely to destroy the tree is liable to a fine in the Magistrates' Court of up to £2,500.

REPLACEMENT OF TREES: ENFORCEMENT

9.14   If a tree in a conservation area is removed, uprooted or destroyed in contravention of section 211 the landowner is placed under a duty to plant another tree of an appropriate size and species at the same place as soon as he or she reasonably can.[116] The same duty applies if a tree is removed because it is dead, dying or dangerous or because it is causing a nuisance.[117] The duty attaches to subsequent owners of the land, although the LPA have powers to dispense with the duty.[118] The LPA may enforce the duty by serving a tree replacement notice under section 207 of the Act (see chapter 11 of this Guide).

---

115   See section 72 of the Planning (Listed Buildings and Conservation Areas) Act 1990.

116   See section 213(1) of the Act.

117   Note that trees protected by a TPO which are removed on grounds of nuisance do not have to be replaced under section 206 of the Act.

118   Section 213(2) and (3) of the Act.

CHAPTER 10

Penalties

Only a sweet and virtuous soul,
Like seasoned timber, never gives;
But though the whole world turn to coal,
            Then chiefly lives.

– George Herbert, from *Virtue*

TWO OFFENCES

10.1   Anyone who, in contravention of a TPO:

(1) cuts down, uproots or wilfully destroys a tree, or

(2) tops, lops or wilfully damages a tree in a way that is likely to destroy it

is guilty of an offence.[119] Anyone found guilty of this offence is liable, if convicted in the Magistrates' Court, to a fine of up to £20,000. In serious cases a person may be committed for trial in the Crown Court and, if convicted, is liable to an unlimited fine.

10.2   In determining the amount of any fine for this offence the Court must have regard to any financial benefit which has accrued, or is likely to accrue, in consequence of the offence.[120]

10.3   It is also an offence for anyone to contravene the provisions of a TPO otherwise than as mentioned in paragraph 10.1 above.[121] For example, anyone who lops a tree in contravention of a TPO, but in a way that the tree is not likely to be destroyed would be guilty of this offence (for the Court's interpretation of what is meant by "destroyed" see paragraph 10.8 below). The penalty in this case is a fine in the Magistrates' Court of up to £2,500. For this offence LPAs should note that the Magistrates' Court cannot deal with a case unless the action is brought within six months from the time the offence was committed.[122]

PROSECUTIONS

10.4   The LPA may receive allegations that a contravention has taken place, or is about to take place, from a range of sources (such as members of the public, tree wardens or local councillors). The LPA should investigate whether or not the allegations are true and may wish to visit the site. The person who has notified the LPA of a contravention should be kept informed of the outcome of the investigation.

---

119 See section 210(1) of the Act.

120 See section 210(3)of the Act.

121 See section 210(4) of the Act.

122 See section 127 of the Magistrates' Court Act 1980.

10.5   Under the Police and Criminal Evidence Act 1984 the Home Secretary has issued a code of practice in connection with, among other things, the questioning of people by police officers.[123] LPAs should be aware that the code is not just for the use of police officers. Section 67(9) of the 1984 Act makes clear that people other than police officers who are responsible for investigating offences or charging offenders must have regard to the code. The code sets out when it is necessary to caution people suspected of committing an offence, and how a caution should be given. The LPA's legal department should be able to advise officers responsible for investigating TPO offences on how the code should be applied in practice.

10.6   LPAs are encouraged to liaise with the Forestry Commission if they believe there has been a contravention of the felling licence provisions of the Forestry Act 1967.

10.7   To bring a successful prosecution the LPA should have sufficient evidence to show that:

(1)   the defendant has carried out, caused or permitted work listed in section 210 of the Act,

(2)   the tree was protected by a TPO, and

(3)   the work was carried out without the LPA's consent.

It may be possible to bring a separate action for each tree cut down or damaged in contravention of the TPO. The defendant may claim that the work was permitted by virtue of one of the statutory exemptions (see chapter 6). If so, the burden of proof to show, on the balance of probabilities, that the work fell within the terms of the exemption is placed on the defendant.

10.8   The Courts have held that you do not have to obliterate a tree in order to "destroy" it for the purposes of the Act. It is sufficient for the tree to be rendered useless as an amenity or as something worth preserving.[124]

10.9   As a general rule it is no defence for the defendant to claim ignorance of the existence of a TPO.[125] Nevertheless, the LPA should ensure that a valid TPO exists, that the tree was clearly protected by it and that they have carried out their statutory functions properly. In one case, the defendant escaped prosecution because his ignorance of a TPO was in fact due to the LPA's failure to place a copy of it for inspection as required by the Regulations.[126]

---

123 *Code of Practice for the Detention, Treatment and Questioning of Persons by Police Officers.* This code is included in the Home Office publication, *Police and Criminal Evidence Act 1984 (s.66): Codes of Practice*, which is available from the Stationery Office.

124 See *Barnet LBC v Eastern Electricity Board* [1973] 1 WLR 430.

125 See *Maidstone BC v Mortimer* [1980] 3 All ER 552.

126 See *Vale of Glamorgan BC v Palmer* (1982) 81 LGR 678.

THIRD PARTIES

10.10   As well as prohibiting the unauthorised cutting down, topping, lopping etc of protected trees, the Model Order prohibits the **causing** or **permitting** of such work.[127] Although there is no mention of the term "causing or permitting" in the Act itself the High Court has held that its inclusion in a TPO is within the powers of the Act.[128] Furthermore, section 44 of the Magistrates' Court Act 1980 provides that any person who "aids, abets, counsels or procures the commission by another person of a summary offence" is guilty of the like offence. However, a landowner has been held not liable for the actions of an independent contractor who had been told not to damage in any way a tree which was the subject of a TPO.[129]

10.11   If the contravention of a TPO is committed by a company section 331 of the Act provides that a director, manager or secretary of the company is guilty of the offence if it can be proved it was committed with their consent, or connivance, or was attributable to their neglect.

RIGHTS OF ENTRY

10.12   The LPA may authorise their officers to enter land to ascertain whether an offence has been committed.[130] Such a right must be exercised at a reasonable hour. Alternatively, a magistrate can issue a warrant enabling a duly authorised officer of the LPA to enter land. A warrant authorises entry on one occasion only, at a reasonable hour (unless the case is one of urgency), and within one month of the issue of the warrant.[131] The LPA officer may be accompanied by other persons as may be necessary and may take away tree and soil samples.[132] The officer must, if required, explain the purpose of the visit and produce evidence of his or her authority to enter the land, and must leave the land effectively secured against trespassers.[133] Anyone who wilfully obstructs the LPA officer from exercising these rights of entry is guilty of an offence and liable, if convicted in the Magistrates' Court, to a fine of up to £1,000.[134]

---

127 See article 4(b).

128 See *R v Bournemouth Justices, ex parte Bournemouth Corporation* (1970) 21 P&CR 163.

129 See *Groveside Homes Ltd. v Elmbridge Borough Council* (1987) 284 EG 940.

130 See section 214B(1)(b) of the Act.

131 See section 214C(1) of the Act.

132 See section 214D(1) of the Act.

133 See section 214D(2) of the Act.

134 See section 214D(3) of the Act.

CHAPTER 11

Replacing Trees

And when the woman saw that the tree was good for food, and that it was pleasant to the eyes, and a tree to be desired to make one wise, she took of the fruit thereof, and did eat, and gave also unto her husband with her; and he did eat.

– Genesis, chapter 3, verse 6

REPLACING PROTECTED TREES AND WOODLANDS

11.1   In addition to the criminal penalties described in chapter 10 of this Guide the Act places a duty on landowners, in certain circumstances, to replace trees and woodlands.

THE DUTY TO REPLACE TREES

11.2   Under section 206(1) of the Act the landowner is under a duty to replace a tree which is removed in contravention of the TPO. Outside woodlands the duty also applies if the tree is removed because it is dead, dying or has become dangerous (for more advice on the replacement of woodlands see paragraph 11.11–11.12 below).

11.3   The duty on the landowner is:

(1) to plant another tree,

(2) of an appropriate size and species,

(3) at the same place,

(4) as soon as he or she reasonably can.

11.4   The duty transfers to the new owner if the land changes hands.[135] When planted, the replacement tree is automatically protected by the original TPO,[136] even if it is a different species, although in these circumstances the LPA may wish to vary the TPO to bring it formally up to date (but see paragraph 11.15 below about the status of a replacement tree planted in accordance with a condition of consent).

11.5   There is no duty to replace one tree with two or more trees. A landowner may well be prepared to replace a large species of tree with two smaller ones, but the LPA have powers only to enforce the duty, which is to plant one tree with one replacement.

---

135 See section 206(5) of the Act.
136 See section 206(4) of the Act.

11.6   "The same place" means the position defined in the TPO by reference to the description in the 1st Schedule and the map.[137] It may not be necessary to insist that the replacement tree is planted in the exact position of the original tree (indeed, it may not be practicable to do so), but the place must at least correspond with the position described in the TPO as shown on the map. In the case of "area orders" the position of each tree is not shown on the map, but in the Secretary of State's view the replacement tree should be planted as near as is reasonably practicable to the position of the original tree.

11.7   The duty on the landowner is to plant the replacement tree as soon as he or she reasonably can. In deciding what this means the LPA should carefully consider the circumstances of the case (such as the number of trees involved or the time of year). It does not necessarily mean a matter of a few weeks. It may be reasonable, for example, for the landowner to wait until the next planting season.

11.8   The Courts have not resolved whether there is a duty to replace trees uprooted or destroyed in strong winds. The Secretary of State considers that the duty does apply in such cases, although the LPA may decide not to enforce the duty depending on the circumstances of the case.

11.9   Anyone proposing to remove a tree on the grounds that it is dead, dying or has become dangerous is advised to give the LPA five days' notice before carrying out the work, except in an emergency. The LPA have powers to dispense with the duty to plant a replacement tree,[138] and any request for such a dispensation should be put to the LPA in writing.

11.10   Under section 213 of the Act the same duty is imposed on the landowner following the removal of trees in a conservation area (see paragraph 9.14).

THE DUTY TO REPLACE WOODLANDS

11.11   The landowner's duty to replace woodlands applies only when trees are uprooted or destroyed in contravention of the TPO.

11.12   In this case the duty on the landowner is:

(1) to plant the same number of trees,

(2) (i) on or near the land on which the trees stood, or

    (ii) on such other land as may be agreed between the LPA and the landowner, and

(3) in such places as may be designated by the LPA.

With woodlands, therefore, there is a degree of flexibility when it comes to settling where the replacement trees should be planted.

---

137 See *Bush v Secretary of State for the Environment* [1988] JPL 108.

138 See section 206(2) of the Act.

ENFORCING THE DUTY: TREE REPLACEMENT NOTICES

11.13   If it appears to the LPA that a duty to replace trees or woodlands has not been complied with, they can enforce the duty by serving on the landowner a notice under section 207 of the Act (a "tree replacement notice"). A tree replacement notice has to be served within four years from the date of the alleged failure to comply with the duty (ie four years from the landowner's failure to plant the trees as soon as he or she reasonably could, not four years from the date of the removal of the trees: see paragraph 11.7 above).[139]

ENFORCING CONDITIONS OF CONSENT: TREE REPLACEMENT NOTICES

11.14   The LPA may also serve a tree replacement notice to enforce any condition of consent granted under a TPO requiring the replacement of trees. Again it must appear to the LPA that the condition has not been complied with, and the notice must be served on the landowner. The notice should make clear that it relates to non-compliance with a condition rather than the duty under section 206 or 213 of the Act.

11.15   The Act does not provide that trees planted in accordance with a condition are automatically protected by the original TPO. Where the felled trees comprise all or part of a woodland and the replacements are planted within the woodland area described in the TPO, the Secretary of State considers that the replacement trees are protected by the TPO. In other cases, though, a fresh TPO may be required to secure the protection of the replacements.

Deciding Whether to Serve a Tree Replacement Notice

11.16   The LPA's power to enforce the replacement of trees is discretionary. Clearly they must be satisfied that the duty exists, ie that the trees were protected by a TPO which was in force at the time they were removed. If the trees were the subject of an "area order", for example, the LPA should satisfy themselves that the trees were present when the TPO was made, and so protected by it.

11.17   In deciding whether to take enforcement action the LPA should consider:

(1)   the impact on amenity of the removal of trees, and whether it would be in the interests of amenity (and, in woodlands, in accordance with the practice of good forestry) to require their replacement;

(2)   whether it would be reasonable to serve a tree replacement notice in the circumstances of the case.

If the LPA decide not to take formal enforcement action they should be prepared to explain their reasons to anyone who would rather like to see some action taken.

11.18   If the landowner applies to the LPA asking them to dispense with the duty, the LPA should give their decision in writing, setting out their reasons.

---

139 See section 207(2) of the Act.

Advice and Discussion

11.19   If the LPA believe, in the circumstances, that replacement trees should be planted, they should first try to persuade the landowner to comply with the duty voluntarily. The landowner may not fully appreciate that there is a statutory duty to replace the trees in question. They should discuss the issue with the landowner, who may in turn appreciate the LPA's advice on a range of matters such as choice of species, their size and location, the best time to plant and good practice generally. If persuasion, discussion and advice fail, the LPA should then consider taking formal enforcement action.

What Must be in the Notice

11.20   In general terms a tree replacement notice should tell the landowner what the LPA believe has given rise to the duty and what must be done to comply with it. In particular the notice should:

(1)   specify the number, size and species of the replacement trees,

(2)   specify where the trees are to be planted,

(3)   specify by when the trees are to be planted. Use as a starting point the date on which the notice is due to take effect, and consider when it would be reasonable to expect the planting to be completed (bearing in mind, for example, the number of trees involved, the location, the time of year etc). Note that the landowner will be able to appeal against the notice on the grounds that the period given to carry out the planting is unreasonable,

(4)   specify a date on which the notice is to take effect. *At least 28 days must be given from the date the notice is served.* This gives the landowner an opportunity to appeal against the notice under section 208 of the Act.

11.21   The notice should state what has given rise to the duty and whether the notice relates to (i) the replacement of a tree protected by a TPO, (ii) the replacement of a tree in a conservation area, or (iii) the planting of a tree in compliance with a condition of consent.

11.22   The LPA are also advised to include in the notice:

(1)   a reference to the relevant TPO or conservation area,

(2)   an explanation of the landowner's right of appeal against the notice,

(3)   an explanation of what will happen if the landowner fails to comply with the notice,

(4)   a contact point in the LPA who can deal with any queries.

A model tree replacement notice is at Annex 11.

Failure to Comply

11.23   Failure to comply with a tree replacement notice is not at present an offence. If a tree is not planted within the period specified in the notice[140] the LPA may go on to the land (there is no requirement to give prior notice to the owner or occupier), plant the trees and recover from the landowner any reasonable expenses incurred.[141] The LPA should remind the landowner before the specified period runs out and make clear that they will use their powers if the notice is not complied with. Anyone who wilfully obstructs someone from using these powers is guilty of an offence and liable, if convicted in the Magistrates' Court, to a fine of up to £1000.[142]

11.24   The Act includes a provision enabling the landowner to recover from any other person responsible for the removal of the original trees:

(1) any expenses incurred while complying with a tree replacement notice, or

(2) any expenses paid to the LPA for planting replacement trees themselves.[143]

11.25   Under the Town and Country Planning General Regulations 1992,[144] sections 276 (power to sell materials removed during work), 289 (power to require occupiers to allow work to be carried out by the owner) and 294 (limit on liability of agents or trustees) of the Public Health Act 1936 are applied to tree replacement notices.

---

140 This period may be extended by the LPA.

141 See section 209(1) of the Act.

142 See section 209(6) of the Act, as substituted by the Planning and Compensation Act 1991.

143 See section 209(2).

144 See regulation 14 (SI 1992, No. 1492).

CHAPTER 12

Appeals against Tree Replacement Notices

"The trees! The trees!"

This shout from the leading carriage eddied back along the following four; and at every window perspiring faces expressed tired gratification.

The trees were only three, and eucalyptus at that. But they were also the first seen by the Salina family since leaving Bisacquino at six that morning. It was now eleven, and for the last five hours all they had set eyes on were bare hillsides flaming yellow under the sun. Never a tree, never a drop of water; just sun and dust. Those desiccated trees yearning away under bleached sky bore many a message.

– Guiseppe di Lampedusa, *The Leopard*

THE RIGHT OF APPEAL

12.1   A person served with a tree replacement notice may appeal to the Secretary of State against it on any of the following grounds:[145]

(1)   that the duty to replace trees or, as the case may be, the condition of consent requiring the replacement of trees, does not apply or has been complied with;

(2)   that in all the circumstances of the case the duty to replace trees should be dispensed with;[146]

(3)   that the requirements of the notice (in relation to the size of the trees or their species, or the period given to comply with the notice) are unreasonable;

(4)   that the planting of trees in accordance with the notice is not required in the interests of amenity or would be contrary to good forestry practice;

(5)   that the place on which the trees are required to be planted is unsuitable for that purpose.

12.2   Where an appeal to the Secretary of State is made, the tree replacement notice is of no effect pending the final determination or withdrawal of the appeal.[147]

---

145 See section 208(1) of the Act.

146 This ground was inserted by section 23 of the Planning and Compensation Act 1991, and does not apply to conditions of consent.

147 See section 208(6) of the Act.

HOW TO APPEAL

12.3   An appeal must:

(1) be made before the tree replacement notice takes effect (this should be specified in the notice),

(2) be made in writing to the appropriate Government Office for the Region (see Annex 1), and

(3) indicate the grounds of appeal and state the facts on which it is based.

There is no fee.

12.4   The Secretary of State cannot extend the period for making an appeal, and so has no jurisdiction to determine late appeals. The appeal must be received, or posted so that, in the ordinary course of post, it would be received *before the date on which the notice is stated to take effect.*

PROCEDURE

12.5   Enforcement appeals are handled in a similar way to those against LPA decisions on applications for consent. They are administered by the appropriate Government Office for the Region (see Annex 1). Both parties have the right to a hearing or local inquiry, but are usually content to have the appeal dealt with under the written representations procedure.

12.6   The time limits for submitting representations, which were introduced by the 1999 Regulations, do not apply to appeals against tree replacement notices. The LPA provide a statement in response to the appeal, which should respond to each of the appellant's grounds of appeal. When all the written representations have been made, a site visit is arranged. The Government Office issue the decision on the Secretary of State's behalf. If the appeal is allowed, the notice may be quashed.

12.7   In dealing with an enforcement appeal, the Secretary of State may correct any defect, error or misdescription in the tree replacement notice. He may vary any of its requirements. He must be satisfied, though, that the correction or variation would not cause injustice to the appellant or the LPA. The Secretary of State may decide a notice is so fundamentally defective that it must be quashed.

COSTS

12.8   Unlike the TPO appeals described in chapter 7 of this Guide (see paragraph 7.17) costs may be awarded in tree replacement notice cases which are dealt with under the written representations procedure. One party may apply for costs on the grounds of the other party's "unreasonable behaviour" which causes unnecessary expense. In written representations cases, the application for costs should be made to the appropriate Government Office for the Region. In the case of a hearing or inquiry, the application should be made to the inspector appointed to deal with the appeal. If a hearing or inquiry is cancelled as a result of one of the party's withdrawal, an application should be submitted to the Government Office.

HIGH COURT APPEAL

12.9   The appellant or the LPA may appeal to the High Court against the Secretary of State's decision on the appeal against the tree replacement notice.[148] This further appeal can only proceed with the Court's permission and can only be made on a "point of law" arising from the decision. Disputes about the Department's inspector's findings of fact may not amount to valid grounds of appeal; nor is the Court likely to consider any new findings of fact.

12.10   Rules of Court provide that the appeal must be made within 28 days from the date of the decision, although the Court has discretion to extend the time limit in exceptional circumstances.[149]

12.11   If an appeal to the High Court is made the effect of the tree replacement notice is suspended until:

(1) the final determination of the proceedings, and

(2) any re-hearing and determination by the Secretary of State.[150]

12.12   The Court may refer the case back to the Secretary of State who, in the light of the Court's opinion, will reconsider the case. The Court will not quash the appeal decision or set aside the tree replacement notice; the intention is that the Secretary of State should be able to correct any error, and in doing so he can reconsider the case afresh.

12.13   Anyone thinking about making an appeal to the High Court is advised to take legal advice about the procedures involved and the likely costs that would be incurred if the appeal failed.

148 See section 289(2) of the Act.

149 See the Rules of the Supreme Court (Amendment) 1992 (SI 1992, No.638).

150 See section 289(4B) of the Act, as inserted by section 6 of the Planning and Compensation Act 1991.

CHAPTER 13

Injunctions

He set his sword point to his chest
And ran at the tree, burying the blade to the hilt,
Then with his last effort pulled it from the wound.

When a lead conduit splits, the compressed water
Jets like a fountain.
His blood shot out in bursts, each burst a heartbeat,

Showering the fruit of the tree –
Till the white fruits, now dyed hectic purple,
Dripped his own blood back onto his body

That spilled the rest of its life, in heavy brimmings,
To the tree roots that drank it
And took it up to the fruits, that fattened darker.

– Ovid, *Pyramus and Thisbe*
(from the *Metamorphoses*, translated by Ted Hughes)

THE POWER TO APPLY FOR AN INJUNCTION

13.1   Under section 214A of the Act,[151] the LPA may apply to the High Court or County Court for an injunction to restrain an actual or apprehended (ie likely) offence under section 210 (contravention of a TPO) or section 211 (prohibited work on trees in a conservation area).

DECIDING WHETHER TO APPLY

13.2   The LPA can apply for an injunction whether or not they have used, or propose to use, their other enforcement powers in the Act. But they must be satisfied it is "necessary or expedient" to apply, so the LPA should consider whether or not other remedies offer an adequate solution to the difficulties they face. Ultimately, it is for the LPA to decide whether to apply for an injunction in the light of their assessment of the seriousness of the offence (whether actual or apprehended).

13.3   The LPA should bear in mind that, if an interim injunction is granted, the Court may require them to give an undertaking in damages to the person named in the Court's order, which means that the LPA may have to pay damages if unsuccessful at the trial when seeking a permanent injunction. But it is not a foregone conclusion that the LPA will be required to give an undertaking in damages; the House of Lords have held that the Court have a discretion not to require an undertaking from a public authority properly exercising their law enforcement functions.[152]

151 Inserted by section 23 of the Planning and Compensation Act 1991.

152 See *Kirklees MBC v Wickes Building Supplies* [1992] 3 WLR 170; [1993] AC 227.

13.4   The LPA may apply for an injunction against a person whose identity is not known. The LPA will have to provide the Court with affidavit evidence of their inability to identify the person within the time reasonably available, and the steps they have taken in attempting to do so. They will also have to describe the defendant to the best of their ability to enable effective service of the injunction (for example by reference to a photograph of the defendant or a name by which the defendant is commonly known, even though it might be an alias).

WILL THE COURT GRANT AN INJUNCTION?

13.5   The decision whether to grant an injunction falls entirely within the Court's discretion. Where an injunction is sought to support the criminal law the Court will exercise caution, and in particular will consider whether or not a defence to the charge exists, before granting an injunction. DOE Circular 10/97 suggests the Court is likely to grant an injunction against a named person if:

(1)   the LPA appear to have taken into account what appear to be the relevant considerations (including the personal circumstances of those concerned) in deciding it is necessary or expedient to apply for an injunction,

(2)   there is clear evidence that an offence under section 210 or 211 has occurred, or is likely to occur,

(3)   injunctive relief is a proportionate remedy in the circumstances.

13.6   A great deal depends, therefore, on the general principles applied by the Court. In *City of London Corporation v Bovis*,[153] a case brought under section 222 of the Local Government Act 1972, the Court said the essential foundation was whether it could be inferred that the unlawful operations would continue unless and until effectively restrained by the law; and that nothing short of an injunction would be effective in doing so. But the Bovis case was decided before the new powers to apply for an injunction were brought into effect by the Planning and Compensation Act 1991, and so the Court might not regard themselves as limited by the previous restrictions.[154]

FAILURE TO COMPLY WITH AN INJUNCTION

13.7   Failure to comply with an injunction can have grave consequences. The Court may, at their discretion, commit the person responsible to a term of imprisonment.

---

153 [1992] 3 All ER 697.

154 See *Harwood v Runnymede Borough Council* (1994) 68 P&CR 300.

CHAPTER 14

Compensation

The trees are coming into leaf
Like something almost being said;
The recent buds relax and spread,
Their greenness is a kind of grief.

Is it that they are born again
And we grow old? No, they die too.
Their yearly trick of looking new
Is written down in rings of grain.

Yet still the unresting castles thresh
In fullgrown thickness every May.
Last year is dead, they seem to say,
Begin afresh, afresh, afresh.

– Philip Larkin, *The Trees*

COMPENSATION IN RESPECT OF THE LPA's DECISION

14.1   TPOs make provision for the payment by the LPA of compensation for loss or damage caused or incurred as a result of:

(1) their refusal of any consent under the TPO, or

(2) their grant of a consent subject to conditions.[155]

14.2   To ascertain whether someone is entitled to compensation in any particular case it is necessary to refer to the TPO in question. It is especially important to note that the compensation provisions of TPOs made on or after 2 August 1999 differ substantially from the compensation provisions of TPOs made before that date.

14.3   No rights to compensation arise for any loss or damage caused or incurred after giving the LPA six weeks' notice of a proposal to remove trees in a conservation area (see chapter 9 of this Guide). But compensation rights could arise later if, in response to the notice, the LPA make a TPO and subsequently refuse an application for consent (or grant it subject to conditions).

TPOs made before 2 August 1999

14.4   Under the terms of a TPO made before 2 August 1999 anyone who suffers loss or damage is entitled to claim compensation unless an article 5 certificate has been issued by the LPA (for more guidance on article 5 certificates see paragraph 6.64–6.71). An appeal to the Secretary of State may be made against an article 5 certificate, and in dealing with such

---

155 See section 203 of the Act.

an appeal the Secretary of State may cancel the certificate. All claims for compensation under these TPOs should be made in the manner set out in the TPO (for further guidance see paragraph 14.6 below).

TPOs made on or after 2 August 1999

Non-Forestry Operations

14.5   In deciding an application for consent under a TPO made on or after 2 August 1999 the LPA cannot issue an article 5 certificate. There is a general right to compensation. However, the TPO includes provisions which are intended to limit the LPA's liability to a fair and reasonable extent, and so the general right to compensation is subject to the following exceptions:[156]

(1)   no claim for compensation can be made if the loss or damage incurred amounts to less than £500;

(2)   no compensation is payable for loss of development value or other diminution in the value of land. "Development value" means an increase in value attributed to the prospect of developing the land, including clearing it;

(3)   no compensation is payable for loss or damage which, bearing in mind the reasons given for the application for consent (and any documents submitted in support of those reasons), was not reasonably foreseeable when the application was decided;

(4)   no compensation is payable to a person for loss or damage which was (i) reasonably foreseeable by that person, and (ii) attributable to that person's failure to take reasonable steps to avert the loss or damage or mitigate its extent;

(5)   no compensation is payable for the costs incurred in bringing an appeal to the Secretary of State against the LPA's decision to refuse consent or grant it subject to conditions.

14.6   A claim for compensation must be made to the LPA within 12 months from the date of the LPA's decision or, if an appeal is made, within 12 months from the date of the Secretary of State's decision.[157] The LPA should treat each claim for compensation on its merits and may wish to arrange a site visit by an appropriately qualified officer to assess the claim. Any question of disputed compensation is referred to, and determined by, the Lands Tribunal (see Annex 1).[158] Reference to the Lands Tribunal attracts a fee of £50.[159]

14.7   In dealing with an application for consent under a TPO the LPA are advised to consider whether any loss or damage is likely to arise in consequence of their decision during the following 12 months, having regard to the reasons given for the application and any reports or other documents submitted by the applicant in support of those reasons. They are advised to bear in mind the limitations to their liability to pay compensation (described in paragraph 14.5 above) and that they are not liable to pay compensation for loss or damage

---

156 See articles 9(2), 9(4) and 9(6) of the Model Order in the 1999 Regulations.

157 See article 9(2)(a) of the Model Order in the 1999 Regulations.

158 See section 205(1) of the Act.

159 Under the Lands Tribunal (Fees) Rules 1996 (SI 1996, No.1021).

incurred before the application for consent was made. If the LPA believe that some loss or damage is likely it does not necessarily follow that they should grant consent; they should merely take this factor into account alongside other key considerations, such as the amenity value of the tree, before reaching their final decision.

Forestry Operations

14.8 Where the LPA refuse consent under a TPO made on or after 2 August 1999 for the felling of woodland in the course of forestry operations, compensation is available only to the owner of the land, as defined in section 34 of the Forestry Act 1967. The amount of compensation payable is limited to any depreciation in the value of the trees which is attributable to deterioration in the quality of the timber in consequence of the LPA's refusal of consent. Claims for compensation in these circumstances are regulated by section 11(3) to 11(5) of the Forestry Act 1967.[160]

COMPENSATION IN RESPECT OF A REPLANTING DIRECTION

14.9 Where:

(1) the LPA give a replanting direction (for more guidance on replanting directions see paragraph 6.72–6.75) to secure the replanting of woodland which is felled in the course of forestry operations, and

(2) the Forestry Commission decide not to make any grant or loan in respect of the replanting

the LPA are liable to pay compensation for any loss or damage caused or incurred as a result of complying with the direction.[161]

14.10 In deciding not to make any grant or loan the Forestry Commission must be satisfied that the replanting direction frustrates the use of the woodland for the growing of timber (or other forest products for commercial purposes) and in accordance with the rules or practice of good forestry.[162] The Forestry Commission must, at the request of the person under a duty to comply with the direction, give a certificate stating the grounds for their decision.[163]

14.11 A claim for compensation must be made within 12 months from the date on which the direction was given or, if an appeal is made, within 12 months from the date of the Secretary of State's decision.[164] The period for making a claim may be extended at the discretion of the LPA. Again any question of disputed compensation is referred to, and determined by, the Lands Tribunal.

160 See articles 9(3), 9(5) and 9(6) of the Model Order in the 1999 Regulations.

161 See section 204(2) of the Act.

162 See section 204(1)(b) of the Act.

163 See section 204(3) of the Act.

164 See section 204(4) of the Act.

ANNEX 1
Contacts

1. DEPARTMENT OF THE ENVIRONMENT, TRANSPORT AND THE REGIONS

RURAL DEVELOPMENT DIVISION 4 (RDD4)

Charlotte Jones
Zone 3/C5
Eland House
Bressenden Place
London SW1E 5DU
Tel: 020 7944 5623
Fax: 020 7944 5589
e-mail: rdd4_trees@detr.gsi.gov.uk

GOVERNMENT OFFICES FOR THE REGIONS

Government Office Eastern Region
Room 137
Heron House
49-53 Goldington Road
Bedford MK40 3LL
Tel: 01234 796251
Fax: 01234 796341
e-mail: lcaudrey.goe@go-regions.gov.uk

Government Office East Midlands
Floor D
The Belgrave Centre
Stanley Place
Talbot Street
Nottingham NG1 5GG
Tel: 0115 971 2485
Fax: 0115 971 2556
e-mail: dbarnett.goem@go-regions.gov.uk

Government Office London
9th Floor
Riverwalk House
157-161 Millbank
London SW1P 4RR
Tel: 020 7217 3398
Fax: 020 7217 3471
e-mail: sporter.gol@go-regions.gov.uk

Government Office North East
Room 906
Wellbar House
Gallowgate
Newcastle upon Tyne NE1 4TD
Tel: 0191 202 3647
Fax: 0191 202 3710
e-mail: gpatrick.gone@go-regions.gov.uk

Government Office North West
Room 1117
Sunley Tower
Piccadilly Plaza
Manchester M1 4BE
Tel: 0161 952 4231
Fax: 0161 952 4255
e-mail: mfarquhar.gonw@go-regions.gov.uk

Government Office South East
1st Floor
Bridge House
Walnut Tree Close
Guildford
Surrey GU1 4GA
Tel: 01483 882508
Fax: 01483 882499
e-mail: madlam.gose@go-regions.gov.uk

Government Office South West
4th Floor
The Pithay
Bristol BS1 2PB
Tel: 0117 900 1882
Fax: 0117 900 1906
e-mail: rmogford.gosw@go-regions.gov.uk

Government Office Yorkshire & Humber
Room 1107
City House
New Station Street
Leeds LS1 4US
Tel: 0113 283 6353
Fax: 0113 283 6657
e-mail: cstenner.goyh@go-regions.gov.uk

Government Office West Midlands
1st Floor
77 Paradise Circus
Queensway
Birmingham B1 2DT
Tel: 0121 212 5183
Fax: 0121 212 6657
e-mail: alidgbird.gowm@go-regions.gov.uk

2. FORESTRY COMMISSION: ENGLISH CONSERVANCIES

NATIONAL OFFICE FOR ENGLAND
Great Eastern House
Tenison Road
Cambridge CB1 2DU
Tel: 01223 314546
Fax: 01223 460699
e-mail: fc.nat.off.eng@forestry.gov.uk

ENGLISH CONSERVANCIES
North West England
Peil Wyke
Bassenthwaite Lake
Cockermouth
Cumbria CA13 9YG
Tel: 017687 76616
Fax: 017687 76557
e-mail: nwe.peilwyke@forestry.gov.uk
Conservator: Mr B K Jones

Northumbria and Yorkshire
Wheldrake Lane
Crockey Hill
York YO1 4SG
Tel: 01904 448778
Fax: 01904 448110
e-mail: fc.nyc.york@forestry.gov.uk
Conservator: Dr R J Britton

Midlands
Central Office
Station Road
East Leake
Loughborough LE12 6LQ
Tel: 01509 582334
Fax: 01509 853886
e-mail: fa.midlands.mrasen@forestry.gov.uk
Conservator: Mr A M Brady

East England
Santon Downham
Brandon
Suffolk IP22 2QZ
Tel: 01842 815544
Fax: 01842 813932
e-mail: fa.easteng.sdownham@forestry.gov.uk
Conservator: Mr B P Easton

Severn Wye & Avon
Crown Offices
Bank Street
Coleford
Gloucestershire GL16 8BA
Tel: 01594 810983
Fax: 01594 810628
e-mail: fa.swa.coleford@forestry.gov.uk
Conservator: Mr W Haslegrave

West Country
The Castle
Mamhead
Exeter
Devon EX6 8HD
Tel: 01626 890666
Fax: 01626 891118
Conservator: Mr K Buswell

South East England
Alice Holt
Wrecclesham
Farnham
Surrey GU10 4LF
Tel: 01420 23337
Fax: 01420 22988
e-mail: fa.see@forestry.gov.uk
Conservator: Mr A J A Betts

3. OTHER ORGANISATIONS

Arboricultural Association
Ampfield House
Romsey
Hants SO51 9PA
Tel: 01794 368717

**Arboricultural Advisory and Information
Service (AAIS)**
Alice Holt Lodge
Wrecclesham
Farnham
Surrey GU10 4LF
Tel: 01420 22022
Tree helpline: 0897 161147

Institute of Chartered Foresters
7A St Colme Street
Edinburgh EH3 6AA
Tel: 0131 2252705

English Nature
Northminster House
Peterborough
PE1 1UA
Tel: 01733 455000

English Heritage
23 Savile Row
London
W1X 1AB
Tel: 020 7973 3000

Association of Professional Foresters
7-9 West Street
Belford
Northumberland NE70 7QA
Tel: 01668 213937

Royal Institute of Chartered Surveyors
12 Great George Street
Parliament Square
London SW1P 3AD
Tel: 020 7222 7000

The Crown Estate
16 Carlton House Terrace
London SW1Y 5AH
Tel: 020 7210 4377

The Lands Tribunal
48/49 Chancery Lane
London
WC2A 1JR
Tel: 020 7936 7200

ANNEX 2

Model Regulation 3 Notice[165]

IMPORTANT – THIS COMMUNICATION MAY AFFECT YOUR PROPERTY

TOWN AND COUNTRY PLANNING ACT 1990
TOWN AND COUNTRY PLANNING (TREES) REGULATIONS 1999

Tree preservation order: [title]
[name of Council]

THIS IS A FORMAL NOTICE to let you know that on [insert date] we made the above tree preservation order.

A copy of the order is enclosed. In simple terms, no one is allowed to cut down, top or lop without our permission any of the trees described in the 1st Schedule of the order and shown on the map.

Some information about tree preservation orders is in the enclosed leaflet, *Protected Trees: A Guide to Tree Preservation Procedures*, produced by the Department of the Environment, Transport and the Regions.

We have made the order because [give reasons].

[The order came into force, on a temporary basis, on [insert date], and will remain in force for six months. During this time we will decide whether the order should be given permanent status.]

People affected by the order have a right to object or make comments on any of the trees or woodlands covered before we decide whether the order should be made permanent.

If you would like to make any objections or comments, please make sure we receive them in writing by [insert date – *give **at least** 28 days from the date of the notice*]. Your comments must meet regulation 4 of the Town and Country Planning (Trees) Regulations 1999 (a copy is attached). Please send your comments to [name and address of LPA officer]. We will carefully consider all objections and comments before deciding whether to make the order permanent.

We will write to you again when we have made our decision. In the meantime, if you would like any more information or have any questions about this letter, please contact [name, address and telephone number of LPA officer].

Dated: [insert date]

Signed: [Council's authorised officer] on behalf of [Council's name and address]

---

165 To be served by LPAs on making a tree preservation order [see paragraph 3.23 of this Guide].

COPY OF REGULATION 4 OF THE TOWN AND COUNTRY PLANNING (TREES) REGULATIONS 1999

Objections and representations

4(1) Subject to paragraph (2), objections and representations:

(a) shall be made in writing and:

(i) delivered to the authority not later than the date specified by them under regulation 3(2)(c); or

(ii) sent to the authority in a properly addressed and pre-paid letter posted at such time that, in the ordinary course of post, it would be delivered to them not later than that date;

(b) shall specify the particular trees, groups of trees or woodlands (as the case may be) in respect of which the objections or representations are made; and

(c) in the case of an objection, shall state the reasons for the objection.

4(2) The authority may treat as duly made objections and representations which do not comply with the requirements of paragraph (1) if, in the particular case, they are satisfied that compliance with those requirements could not reasonably have been expected.

ANNEX 3

Model Letter of Confirmation[166]

TOWN AND COUNTRY PLANNING ACT 1990
TOWN AND COUNTRY PLANNING (TREES) REGULATIONS 1999

Tree preservation order: [title]
[name of Council]

On [date] we made the above tree preservation order, and sent you a copy.

We have considered whether or not the order should be confirmed (or, in other words, made permanent). [Insert number] objections and other comments were made about the order; we considered these before reaching our decision. On [date] the Council decided:

[not to confirm the order.]

[to confirm the order.]

[to confirm the order subject to modifications. A copy of the modified order is enclosed.]

[Set out reasons for the decision.] For more information about our decision, please contact [name, address and telephone number of LPA officer].

[Set out the effect of the Council's decision. Explain (if appropriate) how an application to cut down or carry out work on protected trees can be made.]

[IF ORDER IS CONFIRMED:
If you disagree with our decision you can challenge it by applying to the High Court under sections 284 and 288 of the Town and Country Planning Act 1990. You can apply to the High Court if you believe:

(1) the order is not within the powers of the Town and Country Planning Act 1990; or

(2) the requirements of the 1990 Act or Town and Country Planning (Trees) Regulations 1999 have not been met.

You must apply to the High Court within six weeks from the date of our decision.]

---

166 To be sent by LPAs after reaching a decision on whether to confirm a tree preservation order [see paragraph 3.44 of this Guide].

ANNEX 4

Code of Practice for Utility Operators[167]

This code of practice restates the main points in:

a. Appendix B of DOE Circular 9/95 (General Development Order Consolidation, published May 1995) on **Non-Statutory Consultation and Publicity** in respect of **Development by Statutory Undertakers;**

b. the National Joint Utilities Group's **Guidelines for the Planning, Installation and Maintenance of Utility Services in Proximity to Trees** ("NJUG 10", published April 1995).

It applies to the following utility operators: (1) gas, (2) electricity, (3) telecommunication, including cable communication, and (4) water or sewerage undertakers.

The "precautionary area" means the area around a tree, measured from the centre of the trunk, which is equal to four times the trunk's circumference.[168]

The "tree officer" means the appropriate officer of the local district planning authority.

1. There should be regular informal contact between the utility operator and tree officer in accordance with the advice given in DOE Circular 9/95 (Appendix B, paragraph 8–12). In particular, there should be discussion between the tree officer and utility operator to establish the areas where trees make an important contribution to the quality and enjoyment of the environment. In these areas the utility operator will (except in emergencies) inform the tree officer before carrying out any work on, or within the precautionary area of, trees.

Such areas might include:

- trees known to be protected by TPOs. The tree officer should respond promptly to requests by the utility operator for information on TPOs;

- conservation areas, especially those where trees were a factor in their designation;

- other places which the tree officer considers locally distinctive because of the nature and extent of the tree cover.

---

167 See paragraph 6.24 of this Guide.
168 The circumference of the tree should be measured at 1.5 metres above the natural ground level.

2.   When working on or near trees (above or below ground), the utility operator will follow the guidelines in NJUG 10. In particular:

- excavation with machinery in the precautionary area is totally unacceptable. Wherever possible trenchless techniques should be used. Otherwise, trenches will be dug carefully by hand – retaining as many roots as possible;

- roots over 25mm in diameter will not be cut unless the tree officer agrees beforehand;

- when backfilling trenches, an inert granular material mixed with top soil or sharp sand (NOT builders sand) will be placed around the retained roots and compacted carefully. On non-highway sites, only excavated soil will be used;

- heavy mechanical plant must not be moved or used within the precautionary area, except on existing hard surfaces. In addition, equipment, spoil or building material (including chemicals) must not be stored in the precautionary area;

- if the trunk or branches of a tree are damaged in any way, the utility operator will carry out any remedial tree work recommended by the tree officer.

3.   All tree work will be carried out in accordance with the current British Standard.[169]

169 The current British Standard is BS 3998:1989, Recommendations for Tree Work.

ANNEX 5

Model Tree Work Application Form[170]

---

1. APPLICANT'S DETAILS

Name of Applicant:

Address:

Daytime telephone number:

Name of Applicant's Agent (if applicable):

Address:

Daytime telephone number:

---

2. THE TREE PRESERVATION ORDER

I wish to apply to the Council for consent to carry out work on a tree or trees protected by a tree preservation order.

Title of tree preservation order (if known):

Reference number of tree or trees on the order (if known), eg the oak marked T1:

---

3. THE TREES AND THE APPLICANT'S INTEREST IN THEM

Give the address of the land on which the tree or trees stand (if different from applicant's address given in 1 above):

Is the applicant the owner of the land? YES/NO (delete as appropriate)

If not, specify the applicant's interest in the land (eg occupier, tenant, none etc):

---

170 Form for anyone who proposes to cut down or carry out work on trees protected by a tree preservation order [see paragraph 6.38 of this Guide].

4. THE APPLICATION

Please describe the application by completing the table below.

Specify the tree(s) to which the application relates.

Describe the work you wish to carry out.[171]

Give your reasons for making the application.

TREE(S)	NO. ON PLAN BELOW	PROPOSED OPERATIONS	REASONS

5. PLAN

In the space below, please provide a sketch or street plan showing the location of the tree(s) in relation to surrounding property.

Sign and date your application and send your completed form to [name and address of Council]. The Council will acknowledge your application as soon as possible.

Signed:

Date:

---

171 If you want to carry out work other than felling (for example, pruning or pollarding) please describe what you want to do as accurately as possible. Vague applications will take longer to process.

ANNEX 6

Model Acknowledgement of Application[172]

Tree preservation order: [title]
Application reference number: [ref. no.]

I acknowledge receipt of your application of [date of application] under the above tree preservation order to carry out the following work:

[brief description of work proposed].

Your application was received by us on [date of receipt].

[Set out the Council's arrangements for publicity. For example:

It is our policy to give local bodies and members of the public an opportunity to comment on your application. We write to your local Councillors, Parish Council and local residents asking for their comments to be returned within three weeks. Details of your application can also be inspected at [address, days and hours during which application can be inspected]. All comments are carefully considered before a decision is made.]

An officer of the Council/arboriculturist will visit the site to assess your application.

Most of our decisions are issued within [six weeks]. Our decision will be sent to you, [your agent] [and anyone who sends us written comments about your application].

If we do not give you our decision by [insert specific date, eight weeks or two months from date application was received, depending on the terms of the TPO in question], or any longer period agreed with us in writing, you can appeal to the Secretary of State for the Environment, Transport and the Regions by writing to [address and telephone number of the relevant Government Office for the Region]. You do not have to appeal after this date. We will continue to consider your application and issue a decision as soon as possible. If you disagree with our decision, you will still be able to appeal.

If you would like any further information about your application or our procedures, please contact [name, address and telephone number of LPA officer], quoting the reference number given above.

---

172 To be sent by LPAs when they receive applications to cut down or carry out work on trees protected by a tree preservation order [see paragraph 6.42 of this Guide].

ANNEX 7
Model Refusal Notice[173]

Tree preservation order: [title]
Application reference number: [ref. no.]

I refer to your application of [date of application] under the above tree preservation order for consent to carry out the following work:

[brief description of work].

We have considered your application and have decided to refuse consent for the following reasons:

[set out reasons, which should relate to each of the applicant's reasons for making the application.]

If you would like any further information about our decision please contact [name, address and telephone number of LPA officer], quoting the reference number given above.

YOUR RIGHT OF APPEAL[174]

If you disagree with our decision, you can appeal to the Secretary of State for the Environment, Transport and the Regions. If you want to appeal, you must do so by writing to [address and telephone number of relevant Government Office for the Region] within 28 days from the date you receive this decision.

COMPENSATION[175]

If you suffer any loss or damage as a result of this refusal of consent, you may be entitled to recover from the Council compensation. If you wish to make a claim you must do so within 12 months from the date of this decision (or, if you appeal to the Secretary of State, within 12 months from the date of his decision). Claims should be made in writing to [name and address of relevant officer of the Council].

---

173 To be served by LPAs when refusing applications for consent to cut down or carry out work on trees protected by a tree preservation order [see paragraph 6.61 of this Guide].

174 This paragraph should also be included (with appropriate amendment) where the LPA grant consent subject to conditions.

175 This paragraph should also be included (with appropriate amendment) where the LPA grant consent subject to conditions.

ANNEX 8

Model Article 5 Certificate[176]

CERTIFICATE UNDER ARTICLE 5 OF THE TREE PRESERVATION ORDER

THE COUNCIL CERTIFY in respect of [identify trees, group of trees or woodlands], that they are satisfied:

[their decision is in the interests of good forestry].

[the [trees or woodlands] have [an outstanding] [a special] amenity value].

Our reasons for issuing this certificate are:

[give reasons why decision is in the interests of good forestry].

[give reasons why the trees or woodlands have an outstanding or special amenity value].

The effect of this certificate is to remove our liability to pay compensation for any loss or damage suffered as a result of our decision.

You can appeal to the Secretary of State for the Environment, Transport and the Regions against this certificate by writing to [address and telephone number of the relevant Government Office for the Region] within 28 days from the date you receive it. If your appeal is successful, the Secretary of State may cancel the certificate.

---

176 Sometimes issued by LPAs under TPOs made before 2 August 1999 when giving notice of their decision on an application to cut down or carry out work on trees protected by a tree preservation order [see paragraph 6.71 of this Guide].

ANNEX 9

Model Appeal Statement[177]

Background papers must be sent to the Government Office with the appeal questionnaire, which must be submitted no later than two weeks from the starting date of the appeal. A fuller statement, if the LPA wish to make one, must be submitted no later than six weeks from the starting date.

1. COVERING LETTER

Include the Government Office's reference number for the appeal.

2. THE TREE AND ITS SURROUNDINGS

A description of the tree and its surroundings, restricted to aspects relevant to the appeal.

3. STATEMENT

Additional statement required to clarify or support the LPA's reasons for their decision. This should, if necessary, supplement the reasons already set out in the LPA's decision on the application and comment on new issues arising since the decision. Also enclose the LPA officer's recommendation on the application, if not already provided with the appeal questionnaire.

(For appeals brought against the LPA's failure to determine an application, a more detailed statement will be necessary.)

AVOID:

(1) including in the statement a detailed history of past applications in respect of the tree or trees in the area (anything the LPA consider relevant can be included in the background papers);

(2) including in the statement a detailed history of the application (again, this can be determined from the background papers).

---

177 Format to be followed by LPAs when submitting TPO appeal statements [see paragraph 7.9 of this Guide].

ANNEX 10

Model Acknowledgement of Section 211 Notice[178]

Reference number of notice: [ref. no.]

I acknowledge receipt of your letter of [date of notice] giving us notice that you propose to carry out the following tree work:

[brief description of work proposed].

The [tree or trees] are in the [title of conservation area].

We have six weeks from the date of your letter to consider making a tree preservation order on the [tree or trees]. If by [specific date, six weeks from the date of the section 211 notice] you do not hear from us, you may carry out the work as long as you do so within two years from the date of your letter and do no more work on the [tree or trees] than is set out in your letter. [We will, however, aim to inform you of the outcome of your proposal before this date.]

[Set out the Council's arrangements for publicity. For example:

It is our policy to give local bodies and members of the public an opportunity to comment on your proposal. We write to your local councillors, parish council and local residents asking for their comments to be returned within three weeks. Details of your proposal can also be inspected at [address, days and hours during which notice can be inspected]. Any comments we receive will be carefully considered.]

An officer of the Council/arboriculturist will visit the site to assess your proposal.

If you would like any further information about this letter or our procedures, please contact [name, address and telephone number of LPA officer], quoting the reference number given above.

---

178 To be sent by LPAs when they receive notices to cut down or carry out work on trees in a conservation area [see paragraph 9.8 of this Guide].

ANNEX 11

Model Tree Replacement Notice[179]

IMPORTANT – THIS COMMUNICATION AFFECTS YOUR PROPERTY

TOWN AND COUNTRY PLANNING ACT 1990 (as amended by the Planning and Compensation Act 1991)

TREE REPLACEMENT NOTICE

Tree preservation order: [title]
[name of Council]

1. **THIS IS A FORMAL NOTICE** which is served by the Council under section 207 of the Town and Country Planning Act 1990 ("the Act") because it appears to them that:

    [you have not complied with a duty to plant [a tree/trees] under section 206 of the Act].

    [you have not complied with a condition of consent granted under the above tree preservation order to plant [a replacement tree/replacement trees]].

    [you have not complied with a duty to plant [a tree/trees] in a conservation area under section 213 of the Act].

2. **THE LAND AFFECTED**

    Land at [address of land], shown edged red on the attached plan.

3. **REASONS FOR SERVING NOTICE**

    [On or around [date], a beech tree protected by the above tree preservation order was cut down on the grounds that it had become dangerous. Under section 206 of the Act the owner of the land is under a duty to plant another tree. It appears to the Council that this duty has not been complied with.]

    [On [date], the Council granted consent to fell an oak tree protected by the above tree preservation order subject to a condition to plant a replacement tree or trees [give details of condition]. It appears to the Council that this condition has not been complied with.]

---

179 To be served by LPAs when enforcing any requirement under the Act to replace trees [see paragraph 11.22 of this Guide].

[On or around [date], an ash tree situated in the [title of conservation area] was removed in contravention of section 211 of the Act. Under section 213 of the Act the owner of the land is under a duty to plant another tree. It appears to the Council that this duty has not been complied with.]

[Then set out the relevant facts leading up to the Council's decision to serve the notice, and give reasons for that decision.]

4. WHAT YOU ARE REQUIRED TO DO

You are required to plant [number, species and size of tree or trees to be planted] at the place(s) shown encircled on the attached plan.

Time for compliance: [X months from the date stated in paragraph 5 below.]

5. WHEN THIS NOTICE TAKES EFFECT

This notice takes effect on [insert date, not less than 28 clear days after the date of service], unless an appeal is made against it beforehand.

Dated: [date of notice]

Signed: [Council's authorised officer] on behalf of

[Council's name and address]

YOUR RIGHT OF APPEAL

You can appeal to the Secretary of State for the Environment, Transport and the Regions against this notice by writing to [name of relevant Government Office for the Region]. Your appeal must be received, or posted in time for it to be received, before [insert the date specified in paragraph 5 above]. You can appeal on any one or more of the following grounds:

(1) that the provisions of the duty to replace trees or, as the case may be, the conditions of consent requiring the replacement of trees, are not applicable or have been complied with;

(2) that in all the circumstances of the case the duty to replace trees should be dispensed with in relation to any tree;

(3) that the requirements of the notice are unreasonable in respect of the period or the size or species of trees specified in it;

(4) that the planting of a tree or trees in accordance with the notice is not required in the interests of amenity or would be contrary to the practice of good forestry;

(5) that the place on which the tree is or trees are required to be planted is unsuitable for that purpose.

You must also state the facts on which your appeal is based.

FAILURE TO COMPLY

If you do not comply with this notice, the Council may enter the land, plant the tree(s) and recover from you any reasonable expenses incurred.

ADVICE

If you have any questions about this notice or would like some advice on how to comply with it, please contact [name, address and telephone number of LPA officer].

INDEX

CONSERVATION AREAS

DEVELOPMENT

DUTY TO REPLACE TREES (see REPLACEMENT OF TREES)

ENFORCEMENT (see PENALTIES and REPLACEMENT OF TREES)

EXEMPTIONS FROM TPO CONTROL

FELLING LICENCES

INJUNCTIONS

LOCAL PLANNING AUTHORITIES (LPAs)

LPA APPLICATIONS FOR CONSENT

Application to Secretary of State no longer required (6.76)

LPA's internal procedures (6.78)

Publicising applications (6.77)

Requirement to take into account representations (6.78)

Site notices (6.77)

MAKING & CONFIRMING TPOs

Areas of trees (3.11, 3.17–3.18)

    Drawbacks of area orders (3.17)

    Government advice on use of area orders (3.18)

Confirming TPOs

    Advice on good practice (3.36–3.38)

    Confirming TPOs after six months (3.34)

    Confirming TPOs subject to modifications (3.39–3.40)

    Delay in confirming TPOs (3.34)

    Endorsing TPO at confirmation stage (3.41–3.42)

    Informing people affected of LPA's decision (3.43–3.44)

    LPA's internal procedures at confirmation stage (3.33)

    LPA's powers at confirmation stage (3.32)

Copying TPO to owner/occupier (3.21)

Copying TPO to owner/occupier of 'adjoining land' (3.24)

Groups of trees (3.11, 3.14)

Government advice on making TPOs (3.2–3.5)

High Court challenge of TPO (3.45–3.48)

    Application to High Court must be made within six weeks (3.47)

    High Court's powers (3.47)

Individual trees (3.11, 3.14)

LPA not required to copy TPO to District Valuer and Forestry Commission (3.22)

LPA's internal procedures when making TPO (3.6)

LPA's power to make TPOs (3.1)

Model form of TPO (3.8)

Objections and representations about TPOs

    LPA must take into account objections and representations (3.31, 3.36–3.38)

    Must be delivered by date given in regulation 3 notice (3.29)

    Must be made in writing (3.29)

    Reasons must be given (3.29)

Public inspection of TPOs (3.21, 3.49)

Publicising TPOs (3.28)

Regulation 3 notices

    Contents of regulation 3 notice (3.21)

    Advice on good practice (3.23)

    Serving regulation 3 notices (3.25–3.27)

Rights of entry when making etc TPOs (3.7)

Sealing: LPA not required to seal TPO (3.20)

Secretary of State's power to make TPO (1.6)

Section 201 directions (3.19)

Site visits

    Before making a TPO (3.7)

    Before confirming a TPO (3.35–3.36)

    When considering applications under a TPO (6.33, 6.44)

TPO map: importance of accuracy (3.11–3.13)

'Trees': no statutory definition (2.1)

Trees under good management (3.4)